Convivial
Urban Spaces

Convivial Urban Spaces

Creating Effective Public Places

Henry Shaftoe

publishing for a sustainable future

London • Sterling, VA

First published by Earthscan in the UK and USA in 2008

ISBN: 978-1-84407-388-7
Typeset by Fish Books
Printed and bound in the UK by Cromwell Press, Trowbridge
Cover design by Rob Watts

For a full list of publications please contact:

Earthscan
Dunstan House
14a St Cross Street
London EC1N 8XA
UK
Tel: +44 (0)20 7841 1930
Fax: +44 (0)20 7242 1474
Email: earthinfo@earthscan.co.uk
Web: **www.earthscan.co.uk**

22883 Quicksilver Drive, Sterling, VA 20166-2012, USA

Earthscan publishes in association with the International Institute for Environment and Development

A catalogue record for this book is available from the British Library

Library of Congress Cataloging-in-Publication Data

Shaftoe, Henry.
Convivial urban spaces : creating effective public places / Henry Shaftoe.
    p. cm.
Includes bibliographical references.
ISBN 978-1-84407-388-7 (hardback)
1. Public spaces. 2. City planning—Social aspects. 3. Architecture—Human factors. I. Title.
NA9053.S6S53 2008
711'.4—dc22

                    2008001743

The paper used for this book is FSC-certified and elemental chlorine-free. FSC (the Forest Stewardship Council) is an international network to promote responsible management of the world's forests.

Contents

Acknowledgements

All photographs are by the author, unless otherwise acknowledged.

I would like to thank the following people who have helped, in various ways, with the research and production of this book: Tamsine O'Riordan, Michele Lavelle, Francesc Guillen, Clara Quintana, Lorenzo Segato and Jamie Roxburgh.

CHAPTER ONE

Introduction

This is not just an urban design book, nor is it a social policy book or management guide – in fact it is a bit of all three plus some more. The challenge in creating and maintaining successful public spaces is to achieve an integrated approach, which includes design and management set within the broader context of urban policy. Many books have been written about public space from a design (usually visual) point of view and some books have been written from a policy viewpoint. I have undertaken the rather daunting task of straddling several disciplines, because I feel that only by taking this multifaceted approach will we succeed in producing more convivial spaces. As Ken Worpole, one of the most prolific and perceptive writers about public space, observes: 'Given the deep social and economic nature of the circumstances that underpin or undermine a vibrant community and public space culture, it is clear that design or architecture alone cannot solve these problems, though in many places there is still a pretence that they can' (quoted in Gallacher 2005 p11).

Overview

Why, when we have more overall wealth with which to potentially enrich spaces and places for citizens to enjoy, have we often produced built environments that are bland or ill-conceived for public use and, in some cases, positively unpleasant?

What kind of public spaces do people prefer to be in? This book aims to tease out what gives some places 'personality' and 'conviviality', so that we can learn from the past and present to design, maintain and manage better quality built environments in future.

Drawing on theory, research and illustrated case studies, this book identifies the factors that draw people to certain places. In the 1960s and 70s there was considerable published discussion about what differentiates livable urban environments from unpleasant (and subsequently problematic) ones (see for example Jacobs 1961, Cullen 1961, Rapoport 1977). This important debate about the form and nature of successful spaces and places appears to have been superseded by narrower technical discussions about physical sustainability, security, management and aesthetics.

Many studies of the urban fabric (including a number written by this author) start with an analysis of what is *wrong*, but this book will also look at what is *right* and see if there are any replicable formulas for successful public spaces and places.

Figure 1 Unconvivial: Dublin docks area redevelopment

Figure 2 Unconvivial: Causewayside, Edinburgh

Figure 3 Convivial: Freiburg, Southern Germany

Figure 4 Convivial: Camden Lock, London

Discussion

I have spent most of my professional career working in or visiting the most unpopular and degrading parts of towns and cities, in an (often futile) attempt to help them improve. But in my travels to many towns and cities both here and abroad I have also tried to look at the flip side – what it is about some places that makes me feel good in them?

There has been a recent interest in making 'better public places', emanating both from the British Government (e.g. through their support for the Commission for Architecture in the Built Environment [CABE]) and the built environment professions (e.g. the Urban Design Group). In America, the drive for better place-making is spearheaded by the New York-based Project for Public Spaces

and we now have the European Centre on Public Space driving a similar agenda on this side of the Atlantic. This has led to various guides on 'place-making' (e.g. the *Good Place Guide* and various CABE briefings). But this guidance is based on what professional designers consider a good place. Less research has been undertaken into what ordinary citizens want from their public spaces and what they perceive as good places to be in (i.e. convivial spaces). This book is based on a multidisciplinary understanding of what makes certain public spaces more successful than others and draws on user feedback as well as professional opinion and academic research. I have coined the term 'convivial spaces' to describe open, public locations (usually squares or piazzas) where citizens can gather, linger or wander through. In some cases, such as Stroget

Figure 5 Siena, Italy

(the famous 'walking street') in Copenhagen, streets and their associated open areas can be convivial spaces. 'Convivial' is defined in dictionaries as 'festive, sociable, jovial and fond of merry-making', usually referring to people, but it can equally apply to a situation. Famously, Ivan Illich used the term in the title of his seminal work *Tools for Conviviality*. Places where people can be 'sociable and festive' are the essence of urbanity.

Without such convivial spaces, cities, towns and villages would be mere accretions of buildings with no deliberate opportunities for casual encounters and positive interactions between friends or strangers. The trouble is that too many urban developments do not include such convivial spaces, or attempts are made to design them in, but fail miserably.

However, convivial public spaces are more than just arenas in which people can have a jolly good time; they are at the heart of democratic living (Carr et al 1992) and are one of the few remaining loci where we can encounter difference and learn to understand and tolerate other people (Worpole and Greenhalgh 1996). Without good urban public spaces, we are likely to drift into an increasingly privatized and polarized society, with all its concomitant problems. Despite some improvements in urban development during the last couple of decades, we still produce many tracts of soulless urban fabric that may deliver the basic functional requirements of shelter, work and leisure but are socially unsustainable and likely generators of future problems.

Figure 6 Brent, North London

There are far too many sterile plazas and windswept corners that are spaces left over from another function (such as traffic circulation or natural lighting requirements for tall buildings). This phenomenon is sometimes referred to as 'SLOAP' – space left over after planning. Urban land is at a premium, so in a profit-orientated society, space where people can just loaf around is not seen as a financial priority. Furthermore, contemporary worries about security, litigation and 'stranger danger' result in the urban realm becoming increasingly privatized and controlled.

Some town centres (e.g. Dallas, Texas) and suburbs have more or less given up on informal communal spaces altogether, on the presumed basis that they are costly to manage and might attract the wrong kind of person or usage. This privatized retreat has reached its apotheosis in the 'gated community' where no one, apart from residents and their approved guests, is allowed to enter. Can such places be genuinely described as 'civilized'?

In this book I suggest that there is no single blueprint for a convivial space, but there do seem to be some common elements, which may be broadly categorized under the headings of *physical* (including design and practical issues), *geographical* (location), *managerial, sensual* (meaning how a space directly affects one or more of our five senses) and *psychological* (how the space affects our mind and spirit).

The book is structured to flow from the theoretical and political to the practical. So early sections cover the whys and wherefores of public space before moving on to principles and then some specific proposals and examples.

Defining Convivial Spaces

Francis Tibbalds, in his seminal work *Making People-friendly Towns* (1992), suggests that such places should consist of 'a rich, vibrant, mixed-use environment, that does not die at night or at weekends and is visually stimulating and attractive to residents and visitors alike'. John Billingham and Richard Cole, in their *Good Place Guide* (2002), chose case studies that answered affirmatively to the following questions: 'Is the place enjoyable – is it safe, human in scale, with a variety of uses? Is it environmentally friendly – sunlit, wind and pollution-free? Is it memorable and identifiable – distinctive? Is it appropriate – does it relate to its context? Is access freely available?'

Given that many convivial places seem to have grown organically through an accumulation of adaptations and additions, can we design such places at the drawing board? Critics of formal architecture and planning such as Bernard Rudofsky (*Architecture without Architects* [1964]) and Christopher Alexander (*The Timeless Way of*

Building [1979], *A Pattern Language* [1977]) suggest that we are better off 'growing' good places and spaces, rather than trying to build them from a blueprint – this is discussed in 'Designed or Evolved?' in Chapter 4 (page 81). There are some ancient and modern examples to suggest that it *is* possible to design convivial places as a whole, but they tend to be relatively small in scale. The post-1947 culture of master-planning whole urban areas is less likely to accommodate the fine grain, local nuance and adaptability that seem to be at the root of convivial places.

You may disagree with me about the kind of places that are convivial; *you* may enjoy the buzz of a much more hard-edged, clean and symmetrical environment, such as Canary Wharf (London) or La Défense (Paris). You may even enjoy spending time wandering around the closely supervised and sanitized spaces of out-of-town shopping malls such as Cribbs Causeway near Bristol and Bluewater in Kent; many do, but for what reasons? And why do other people loathe such places? There are many such questions to be answered about the effect of different places on different people.

The rest of this book attempts to unpack the various factors and observations, outlined above, that constitute convivial spaces. By understanding what the ingredients of a successful public space are, we should be able to create more good ones, avoid constructing more bad ones and remedy some of the already existing bad ones. I recognize that good urban design is a crucial factor in all this, but unlike many books on the subject, I also stress the significance of management and geography and how all these objective factors affect our senses and psychology. Ultimately, conviviality is a subjective *feeling*, underpinned by, but not to be confused with, the actual physical state of a place.

This book is not an exercise in cosy nostalgia. Examples will be given of comparatively recent 'unplanned' places that have considerable 'personality' and recent developments or redevelopments that have transcended the sterility of many modern built environments. Although arguing for a more humane approach to urban development that encourages positive social interaction, this is not based only on the author's whims but aims to be scientifically balanced and academically rigorous, based on a multidisciplinary understanding of the functioning and perception of the built environment, drawing on theory and research from environmental psychology, sociology, anthropology and urban design.

Because of my background, experience and cultural heritage, I mostly refer to urban spaces in Europe. It could be claimed that Europe has the longest history and most sophisticated experience of designed public spaces (from classical Greece and the Roman Empire onwards), but this would be to downplay the importance of public spaces in all cultures and civilizations. Africa, India and the Far East all offer historic examples of fine and popular public spaces, suggesting that the need for convivial space is fundamental to human nature:

You will also notice that many of the photographs of people's behaviour in public spaces have been taken in my adopted home town of Bristol. This is purely opportunistic insofar as I regularly have reason to walk through the streets and squares of Bristol and I always carry a camera in case of a chance encounter. And as Edmund Bacon (1975) says: 'Only through endless walking can the designer absorb into his being the true scale of urban spaces' (p20). I would argue that the way people use the public spaces of Bristol are not fundamentally different to how they would use them in Newcastle or Rotterdam, for example, so I am not apologetic about using so many images from my locality.

What follows is therefore a primarily British-focused, Eurocentric influenced, but I hope not xenophobic, account of urban public space.

Figure 7 Marrakech, North Africa

Source: Kathryn Smith

Figure 8 Campo Santa Margarita, Venice – European conviviality exemplified

In terms of structure, the book aims to flow from the theoretical and general to the practical and specific. However, with such a multifaceted subject, there is bound to be some overlapping and arbitrary ordering of information and discussion. One thing that will become immediately apparent is the sheer number of photographs – a deliberate ploy, on the basis that photographs can often tell you much more about public space than any amount of text could. I also hope that you will find inspiration (or in some cases warning) from the sheer wealth of fascinating public spaces that proliferate in so many countries. You will note that (with the exception of some photos of unsuccessful spaces) nearly all the photographs have many people in them.

Figure 9 Oval Basin: part of the new Cardiff Bay redevelopment – nice big space, but where are the people?

This, to me, is the 'litmus test' of conviviality – successful spaces have people lingering in them. Ultimately, public spaces are about *people*. This may sound like a platitude, but there are still administrations and designers who do not keep this as their central focus, with the result that we end up with impressive or monumental spaces that are mostly empty or underused. What a waste of space!

The main body of the book is divided into three sections. The first section argues the case for having public space and discusses the social policies that affect the kind of public spaces we have. The second section covers the theories and principles that influence the way we design and manage public spaces. The third section aims to be a more practical one, suggesting how we might apply our knowledge to create or maintain 'convivial urban spaces'. The five case studies aim to illustrate many of the points raised in the various sections.

CHAPTER TWO

Public Spaces – Why Have Them and Who Are They For?

Public Space is the playground of society;
the public realm is the playground in which society reinvents itself.

Bunschoten 2002 p6

Why Have Public Space and Who Is It For?

Reports of the death of public space have proven to be premature. As Kayden (2005) notes: 'Corporeal public space has of late taken something of an intellectual beating in a world currently fascinated by cyber-public-space and chastened by declining civic virtues. Academic conferences now ask the question, is public space dead? Yet any observer of city streets and sidewalks understands that urban residents, employees and visitors are not ready just yet to abandon physical space for more esoteric worlds' (p136). Indeed it could just be *because* of the ascendancy of virtual realities such as Sim City and Second Life that people crave real encounters with other real people in real environments. After all, humans are a highly sociable species, on the whole, and the company of others seems to be fundamental to our sense of existence and belonging. However sophisticated the

simulations of cyberspace become, they are unlikely to be a total substitute for the buzz and unpredictability of real life being played out 360 degrees around you.

I should clarify what I intend to concentrate on in this book. Public urban space can cover a wide variety of situations, including libraries, community centres and parks (see for example Mean and Tims 2005). However, I intend to concentrate predominantly on small-scale open spaces in towns – squares, piazzas, plazas, pocket parks and some kinds of street – the kind of places that William Whyte (1980) focused on for his groundbreaking study in New York. I am conscious that for a public space to be real it has to be *used*. As Worpole and Greenhalgh (1996) point out, many designers and architects regard public space as the publicly owned empty bits between buildings. Many of these spaces are useless or dangerous and abandoned, with the result that 'this renders their definition as public space null and void' (p14).

Why, if public spaces are so potentially problematic, do we bother to have them at all? This is where we enter the big concerns of social policy. In an increasingly privatized world, driven by free-market economics, indeed public space can be seen as somewhat of a liability, unless it can be used as a locus for selling and consumption. However, many commentators over the years (including Lewis Mumford, Richard Sennett and Ken Worpole, to name but a few) have claimed that successfully functioning public space is fundamental to the furtherance of democracy and civilized life. Indeed Worpole and Greenhalgh (1996) claim that: 'Public space, we would argue, is now of central political importance to questions of sustainable, equitable and enriching urban life' (p25).

Large claims indeed – surely public spaces are no more than that – places where the general public are allowed? But it has been noted by many that public spaces are important for health, wellbeing, learning, conflict resolution, tolerance and solidarity, to mention but a few benefits. Little wonder that governments from the extremes of the political spectrum, whether totalitarian or free-marketeers, find public space potentially problematic.

Health and wellbeing

Urban public spaces offer obvious health benefits insofar as city residents and workers can get fresh air and exercise in them. This requirement for healthy spaces accessible to urban residents and workers is becoming critical in the light of increasing levels of heart disease and obesity, resulting from more sedentary lifestyles (National Heart Forum et al 2007, Ward Thompson and Travlou 2007). There is also a suggestion that they can promote mental health and wellbeing too (see for example Guite et al 2006, Greenspace Scotland 2004). Possibly as a result of our evolutionary heritage, humans seem to need both social contact with others and some access to greenery in order to maintain psychological balance (see Wilson 1984, Kellert and Wilson 1993), both being provided by good public spaces. This is presumably why people go mad when held in solitary confinement and why this is used as the cruellest form of punishment. There is a growing view that the success of good social policy should not be measured by economic gains but by improvements in wellbeing and happiness of citizens (Layard 2005). Finbar Brereton and colleagues at University College Dublin, have found that 'environmental and urban conditions' are critical to people's sense of wellbeing: 'Location specific factors are shown to have a direct impact on life satisfaction' (Brereton et al 2006 p2). Therefore well-designed and well-managed public spaces could contribute to overall happiness – surely a satisfactory end in itself and the ultimate goal of enlightened policy?

Learning

Insofar as effective public spaces are arenas for the 'theatre of everyday life' they offer considerable social learning opportunities.

Because by definition they are universally accessible, they offer one of the few opportunities for people to directly encounter other people with different norms, behaviours and cultures. So, for example, in the same city-centre space, skateboarders may be observed by office workers on their lunch-break and people of different ethnicities and abilities can share a bench.

People can thus learn about what makes up their society and how other people can have different attitudes, backgrounds and values. This contrasts markedly with the experience of (for example) visiting an IKEA store in an out-of-town shopping mall where one mixes with a homogeneous but segmented part of the population.

In the more formal sense of 'learning', public spaces are often used as arenas for education (field visits) and research (the ubiquitous interviewer with a clipboard, found in so many urban spaces).

Conflict resolution, tolerance and solidarity

Elsewhere in this book there is discussion about the positive aspects of encountering difference and potential conflict in public space, but suffice to say at this point that tolerance comes from close encounters with other citizens, rather than stereotyping them from monocultural enclaves. Public spaces also offer opportunities to build up a sense of solidarity with your fellow citizens, both through ad-hoc encounters and through organized events such as festivals and demonstrations.

Figure 10 Barcelona, Spain

Figure 11 St Enoch's Square, Glasgow

Economic benefits

So much urban policy seems to be driven these days by the desire to make profits that it can be refreshing to claim that public spaces are worth having for purely non-fiscal reasons. However, convivial places can also generate financial benefits, both directly through sales of refreshments, market produce and so on, but also indirectly by making the towns where they are located more popular visitor attractions. The transformation of city centres such as Melbourne in Australia (Gehl and Gemzoe 2001) and Glasgow in Scotland and their subsequent increases in tourist visits are at least partly attributable to improvements in their public spaces. In its 2004 reports 'Please Walk on the Grass' and 'Does Money Grow on Trees?' CABE Space argues that, as well as social and environmental value, good public spaces increase property values and are good for business.

Urban security

A later chapter will go into detail about crime and safety in public spaces, but at this stage it is worth pointing out that well-used convivial places are the alternative to downtown areas abandoned to criminals and the socially rejected, as has happened in a number of US cities. This is based on the theories of having 'eyes on the street', first espoused by Jane Jacobs (1961) and the presence of 'capable guardians' (see Felson and Clarke 1998), i.e. crimes are less likely to occur if potential offenders are aware that there are law-abiding citizens in the area who could witness, report or intervene.

Democracy

In democratic societies, public spaces are the gathering places where the citizenry can express their solidarity and also dissent. They are the locations for demonstrations, pamphleteering and soapbox orations; so important for grassroots democracy. As Denis Wood (1981) points out, public spaces, particularly the less surveyed ones, are where change is fermented and where countermeasures are formulated. No wonder that totalitarian regimes try to control the use of public space by heavy policing, surveillance and curfews. Famous public spaces in non-democratic states (such as Tiananmen Square, Beijing, Red Square, Moscow and Plaza de la Revolución, Havana) tend to be huge and intimidating, apparently expressing the power of the ruling regime and the insignificance of individual citizens.

History, politics and the law

I do not intend to reiterate the history of public spaces, when others have done it well already (see for example Bacon's 1975 work and Moughtin's 1992 introductory chapter); suffice to say that, at least since the ancient Greek *agora*, open public places have been at the heart of civilized urban life. Indeed, the quality and extent of urban spaces could be used as a litmus test for the state of various societies' political health (think of the great parks of London in the 18th century and the reclaiming of Copenhagen's streets for pedestrians in the 20th century.) Because they are so important in civic life, public spaces have also been subject to various laws and controls, both positive and negative. Positive legislation that has helped to further the provision of public space includes the British 'section 106' clause, which allows local authority planning departments to negotiate the provision of public space as a condition of awarding planning permission to developers, and the similar New York 'incentive zoning' scheme (see Kayden 2005). Less encouraging legislation usually centres around the control of public spaces by the use of surveillance, dispersal orders, exclusion orders, loitering laws and curfews.

In summary, small urban public spaces have huge social, political and economic value. The extent to which any town contains suitably convivial spaces is a reflection on how civilized it is.

Securing an Exclusive or Inclusive Urban Realm

A crucial influence on whether people will use or avoid urban public spaces is the degree to which they feel safe in them. The actual risk of becoming a victim of crime is usually less than the fear people feel, but it is the latter that can lead to avoidance. Ironically the people who are least at risk of street crime (older people and women, for example) tend to be the most fearful, while young men, those most at risk, are less fearful (or at least pretend to be!) (see Shaftoe 2004). The consequence of all this is that certain public spaces become monoculturally dominated – Saturday nights in town centres, or parts of parks for example – which undermines the intention for public spaces to be democratic places for all. It can also lead to a self-fulfilling prophecy as, in the absence of the moderating presence of a broad mix of citizens, certain places at certain times become arenas for drunken confrontation and intergroup conflict.

Currently there is a debate about whether we should be providing *exclusive* or *inclusive* built environments as a means of promoting urban security. On one side are the 'designing out crime' proselytizers who seek closure and limitation of use of spaces; on the other side are the New Urbanists, Urban Villagers and 24 Hour City people who want to 'crowd out crime' through mixed use and maximizing activity in public areas.

This debate has become more salient since the publication of a raft of government-sponsored reports aimed at informing practitioners about how to revitalize our towns and cities. The reports emanating from the Urban Task Force (1999) and the government quango CABE Space (2005) come down firmly in favour of *inclusive* urban design as a means of achieving safer public spaces, whereas the joint ODPM/Home Office-sponsored publication '*Safer Places*' (2004) is much more equivocal, trying (not entirely successfully, some have argued) to reconcile inclusive with exclusive approaches to urban security.

Certain assumptions are made in this debate, about the degree of influence different styles of urban development can have on crime and offending. This section will set the debate within the broader context of the links between urban design, human behaviour and other social factors that may affect levels of crime and feelings of security in the public realm. Ultimately there are political choices to be made about how we invest in development and regeneration that will determine whether we end up with a predominantly exclusive or inclusive urban realm.

Spot the difference

Both the photographs on this page are of public squares in medium-sized provincial cities. One is a safe place to be in; the other is hostile and the scene of considerable crime and incivilities. The differences between these pictures offer a stark illustration of the links between urban security, quality of life and the built environment. A 'reading' of these two images could suggest that urban security is about context (geographical), context (socio-economic) and context (cultural). This is because, although both squares are about the same size, surrounded by shops and provided with communal facilities, there are some crucial differences that need contextual explanation. Figure 12 is a peripheral housing estate in Bristol while Figure 13 is of a square in the heart of an ancient city (Dijon). The Dijon square welcomes a mixed population of shoppers, visitors and loafers, while the Bristol square is only likely to be used by local people living on one of the most disadvantaged estates in the city. Attempts to redesign the Bristol square (with new shutters, shopfronts, CCTV for safety and a public seating area) have simply not succeeded in the face of overwhelming deprivation in the surrounding area.

What can be deduced from these pictures alone challenges the notion, proselytized by the adherents of crime prevention through environmental design (CPTED) (see Saville 1996), that you can simply 'design out crime' either in a hard (physical security) or soft (natural surveillance via new urbanism) way. Once you have looked at the wider geographical, social, economic and demographic context of any built location, you realize that there are huge variations in motivations and likely reasons to commit crime.

Figure 12 Knowle West, Bristol

Figure 13 Place François Rude, Dijon

Design to keep out or bring in?

Given this problem of 'context', what design and management policies should we be adopting to make public spaces safer? Or is design irrelevant? I don't think it is, but it is the indirect results of design, such as desirability and the types of usage it facilitates, that seem to have as much effect as direct things like target-hardening and surveillance. However, this topic area has been both under-evaluated and mired in political debate about what kind of places we want.

Despite the government's promotion of inclusive urban places, often through the Commission for Architecture and the Built Environment (CABE) (see for example ODPM 2002, CABE 2004a), on the ground the default drift seems to be towards closure, fortification and exclusion. The proliferation of gated spaces (see Atkinson and Blandy 2006), CCTV and private security are all evidence of this exclusive drift. It should be noted too that shopping arcades and malls are the gated communities of commerce, with all the pluses and minuses that this implies (see Gold and Revill 2000).

And the designing out crime brigade are on the offensive (see for example Town and O'Toole 2005). There has been some research into the effectiveness of designing out crime that claims positive outcomes (see for example Armitage 2000) and obviously, all other things being equal, secured by design (SBD) developments will be less victimized than non-SBD ones but, in the real world of urban polarization, *all other things* rarely are equal.

The alternative consists of the development of permeable environments with mixed use and plenty of public spaces, in a deliberate attempt (using concepts such as 'the Urban Village' and 'place-making') to build social capital and a sense of community (see Neal 2003). The trouble is that the security benefits of such inclusive urban spaces have been hardly researched at all. We are mostly relying on gut feeling and faith.

Figure 14 Shopping mall, South Gloucestershire

Inclusive public space – why bother?

Given the previous comments about the obvious security improvements achieved through fortification and enclosure, why should we trouble ourselves with creating or maintaining public spaces and permeable neighbourhoods? Why not just seal everything off and discourage people from wandering around or hanging about in urban areas? To some extent this is what is happening in parts of the US and South Africa, for example; and through the use of dispersal orders and curfews in the UK, the police now have powers to exclude young people in particular from streets and public spaces. However, there is a strong and well-established argument to the contrary – that the safest places are well-populated with both users and casual passers-by who provide more 'eyes on the street' to informally police public spaces (Jacobs 1961, Gehl 2003). As Roger Evans recently stated (2006) 'When a society stops policing itself, it has failed. If everyone in a society can't enjoy all the public spaces within a town then it can't police itself. In order to achieve that, we need a public realm … which is inclusive' (p33).

The argument in favour of inclusive public spaces goes considerably beyond a narrow focus on security to include health, wellbeing and even the very nature of 'civilization'. Richard Sennett (1986) has argued that 'people grow only by the processes of encountering the unknown' (p295) and the best places to encounter difference and the unfamiliar are public spaces, where all segments of society can cross paths, mingle and be observed. Without this observation and engagement with 'difference', Sennett claims in his book *The Uses of Disorder* (1973), we are in danger of becoming increasingly prejudiced and narrow-minded, as we only choose the company of like-minded individuals in our increasingly cocooned daily routines.

Figure 15 Bristol

In a similar vein Louis Mumford (1964) asserted that the function of city public spaces is '… to permit, indeed to encourage, the greatest possible number of meetings, encounters, challenges, between various persons and groups, providing as it were a stage upon which the drama of social life can be enacted, with the actors taking their turn, too, as spectators' (p173). William Whyte (1988) claims that the increases in private travel and electronic communication, rather than turning us in on ourselves, have actually stimulated a greater need for face-to-face contact. We are, after all, a social and sociable species and we need affirmative interaction with other humans for our health and wellbeing.

Finally, there is an economic argument in favour of reviving public space. More people on the streets and in squares means more footfalls past and into shops and cafes. Because 'people attract people', cities with a lively public realm are more likely to appeal to tourists and other visitors. The transformation of Melbourne's public spaces (see Gehl and Gemzoe 2001) is a case in point.

Convivial spaces versus hostile places

Jan Gehl (2003), an eloquent supporter of urban public spaces, argues that 'the disintegration of living public spaces and the gradual transformation of the street areas into an area that is of no real interest to anyone is an important factor contributing to vandalism and crime in the streets' (p78). The CABE *Manifesto for Better Public Spaces* (2004a) claims that: 'Many parks and streets are so derelict and run down that people feel scared to use them. In contrast, places that are well designed and cared for feel safer and people tend to use them more.' So how do we stop the disintegration of public spaces and design or 'grow' new ones? More fundamentally, can 'design' (in the physical layout sense) determine or influence the degree to which a particular urban space is inclusive or exclusive?

Much current policy and practice emanating from the British Government's crime reduction mandate seems to regard public space as a mere arena where various control measures are imposed. The outcome of this is a series of exclusionary initiatives encouraged by the Home Office (ranging from legal controls, such as alcohol bans and dispersal orders, to increased surveillance through CCTV and police community support officers) which sometimes seem to be at odds with the more inclusive 'urban renaissance' policies espoused by the Department for Communities and Local Government (formerly the ODPM). It is intriguing (and perhaps significant) that this dichotomy is a mirror of the conflicting debate in academic and practitioner circles about inclusion or exclusion in urban design and security. It could be argued that this is a realistic response, whereby control measures using deployment of personnel, formal surveillance and legal sanctions have to be used to compensate for 'bad' physical infrastructures that would be too costly to ameliorate. Such an argument has been used in the past to legitimize intense housing management of poorly designed high-rise council estates (DoE 1993), but it is not clear whether it is a justifiable argument for more oppressive control of the public realm.

The extent to which we have gone down a path of exclusion and formal control, as opposed to designing in good behaviour, is elaborated below.

Deployment of personnel

The traditional way of keeping 'undesirables' out of public space, whether these be potential criminals, vagrants, people who are 'different', or just other people's children, is to put someone in a uniform and send them out on patrol. This was done even before the police were formed and has seen a recent revival with the increasing use of private security firms, street wardens and police

Figure 16 Brent, North London: Chalkhill Estate, now demolished

community support officers. In some affluent areas, standard police patrolling has been augmented by private security personnel, paid for by residents' subscriptions and some shopping malls pay a supplement to the local police force to pay for extra patrolling. There is now a better understanding, in some quarters, that merely 'moving people on' is not really solving anything. Cities such as Coventry and Sheffield have employed uniformed 'ambassadors' whose job is to provide a welcome and reassurance to visitors as much as it is to deter offending.

Uniformed patrolling is, at best, a reassurer and a fear-reducer and may act as a deterrent to the would-be offender, assuming that the perceived surveillance is comprehensive enough. At worst, uniformed patrolling is a purely repressive measure where anyone lingering in public space is regarded as a suspicious person and undesirables are hounded out of sight.

Electronic surveillance

Electronic security surveillance could be termed 'armchair patrolling'. Instead of having distinctively clothed people walking around an area, there are distinctively boxed electronics surveying an area, while the control person reclines in their televisual eyrie. The users of public spaces are made aware (through signs on poles and lamp-posts) that their every move is being videotaped to be used as potential evidence against them, so they (supposedly) refrain from doing anything that could render them liable to prosecution.

An approach to security based on electronic surveillance attracts exactly the same caveats as those mentioned above for uniformed patrolling. Furthermore, because of its technological intricacy, it is vulnerable to breakdown, malfunction or malicious damage. Overall CCTV schemes have produced mixed results in terms of crime reduction (Welsh and Farrington 2002, Shaftoe 2002).

Figure 17 City-centre ambassadors, Sheffield

At best CCTV can extend the reach of the guardians of communal public spaces and can offer a protective ring of security until a problem can be sorted out by appropriate personnel. At worst it can become an intrusive, humiliating and repressive means for controlling excluded populations. (See Lyon 1993, Fyfe and Bannister 1998, Williams et al 2000.)

Legal controls

For surveillance and security personnel to be able to sweep offenders and undesirables off the streets, they will need to call on legal sanctions. At one end of the legal spectrum there are police powers to stop and search people suspected of behaving offensively, move on loiterers, and arrest people for causing an obstruction. At the other end there are civil remedies (e.g. for noise control), by-laws and licensing restrictions which can be invoked by local authorities to 'clean up' the streets. Coventry was the site of the first by-law banning the consumption of alcohol in town-centre streets and public spaces (Ramsay 1989, 1990) and since then such street drinking bans have spread exponentially, particularly in response to moral panics about street beggars, loutish behaviour and binge drinking. Such legal and licensing measures do appear to have had an effect in reducing crime and particularly antisocial behaviour in town centres, but one has to ask if the problem has not been moved elsewhere, to sites such as parks just outside the city centre, as appears to have been the case with Coventry.

Another approach to stamping out undesirable behaviour in public spaces was to rigorously enforce the law right down to the most minor infraction, in the belief that intolerance of small delinquencies would prevent the commission of bigger offences. This zero tolerance approach gained huge populist support for a short time in the late 1990s, but its effectiveness as a sustainable approach to controlling antisocial behaviour and nuisance in the streets was soon challenged. For example, Morgan and Newburn (1997) questioned the approach on the grounds of practicality – a lack of police resources and competing demands to tackle serious crime. The approach was also challenged by Young (1998), who suggested a number of other circumstances and factors that might have influenced crime reductions.

Physical barriers

Along with surveillance and legal controls of the types mentioned above, the main way of controlling space in order to minimize the opportunities for crime has been the installation of actual barriers to separate potential offenders from potential victims or their property. The appropriate use of security doors, locking systems, walls, fences, grilles and shutters can all contribute to a safer built environment (Crouch et al, 1999).

If you keep criminals away from their targets (by deterrence or fortification), of course you will reduce some types of crime (notably burglary, vandalism and vehicle crime), but at what expense to the liberty and freedom of movement of law-abiding individuals? Do we want to scuttle from our fortified domestic enclaves to intensively patrolled shopping malls in our centrally locked cars? (see Davis 1992, Ellin 1997). Some people seem to prefer this exclusive kind of security (particularly in North America), but of course you need a certain level of wealth to be able to enjoy it.

Management

Most of the measures described above have attempted to deal with the problem of crime and insecurity through a greater or lesser degree of exclusion and repression. In other words the potential offender has been made unwelcome and the offence has been made more difficult to commit. As already indicated, the risk with these measures is that the problem will move to a different place or change to a different type of crime, as no attempt has been made to deal with the motivation to commit crime or to engage with those likely to offend.

In reality, there are very few career criminals; people who commit offences often do so out of boredom, frustration, desperation or as a by-product of a personal problem such as addiction, psychopathology or homelessness. For even the most hardened recidivist, the criminal act is only a very occasional part of their daily life. Many 'offenders' are bored young people who would engage in more legitimate pursuits if they were given the chance (Graham and Smith 1994).

Instead of excluding undesirables and creating, in the process, an environment that is undesirable to everyone, there is a current move towards making our streets and town centres more attractive, in the hope that crime and antisocial behaviour will be 'crowded out' by the range of legitimate activities and the behavioural norms of the majority of law-abiding citizens (Bianchini 1994). At the same time, it is important to engage with the minority who are displaying unwelcome or desperate behaviour – they may need help, diversion or intensive support.

Enlightened strategic management of town centres and public spaces can make them more attractive, livable and vital, at the same time reducing the density (if not the actual number of incidents) of crime and antisocial behaviour. Programmes that only focus on crime reduction may be too narrow most of the time and there is the risk that they impoverish the urban realm. This revitalization of streets and public areas in Britain is being spearheaded by Town Centre Managers (see www.atcm.org). Although their primary focus is to improve the economic fortunes of town centres, these managers are aware that crime and insecurity are big disincentives to potential users (KPMG/SNU 1990, Coventry Safer Cities 1992).

It should be pointed out that management strategies can also be devised to *exclude* people, or certain categories of people, by either discouragement or actual prohibition, using by-laws or other social controls.

Integration and absorption

The notion of inclusion and neutralization of crime and insecurity described in the management approach above can be taken one step further. As intimated before, 'criminals' are usually people with needs or difficulties who happen to be hanging around in public spaces because they have nowhere else in particular to go. Therefore it is quite possible to engage with such people to help them meet their underlying needs or resolve their difficulties, thus diverting them from crime and antisocial behaviour. In Britain this approach has offered some promising innovations, although they have generally been piecemeal, relying on charitable initiative and local goodwill. Often their primary aim is humanitarian, but with crime prevention or disorder reduction as an added bonus. Examples include the alcohol-free bar run by the Salvation Army in central Swindon, the Centrepoint Shelter for homeless runaways in Soho, London, and even the Big Issue magazine sold by the homeless as an alternative to begging. In some continental European countries this integrative approach to crime and disorder reduction holds greater sway. For example, in Lille, France, a group of delinquents who used the entrance to a metro station as their operating base were contacted by a team of detached youth workers. As a result, they made a video about youth problems in the city centre and most of them were helped by social workers to reintegrate into normal community life (King 1988). A project in Rotterdam, Holland, recruited young people who were loitering and intimidating shoppers in a central street

and offered them a meeting place, support and activities in an adjacent building (Safe Neighbourhoods Unit 1993). In the USA, the Travelers and Immigrants Aid of Chicago operated the Neon Street Clinic, where homeless and runaway young people could receive comprehensive advice and assistance from a range of professionals, or just 'hang out' somewhere warm and dry until they were ready to use the services available (Dryfoos 1990).

Animation

By 'animation' I mean anything that brings public spaces to life in a positive way. Busking, pavement cafes, street festivals and so on all bring more people into the public arena with the belief that they will be extra 'eyes on the street' to improve the feeling of safety and security for other users. Another major attempt at animating our public spaces is to temporally extend their use round the clock and for all sections of the urban community. The '24 Hour City' concept is a relatively new approach to revitalizing streets and town centres (Montgomery 1994, Comedia 1991, Bianchini 1994). A review of British initiatives (Stickland 1996) showed that improving night-time safety was the principal reason for introducing the 24 Hour City concept. Increased safety is seen to derive from improved natural surveillance provided by increases in the numbers and range of people using the streets, including older people who are otherwise less in evidence after dark. The 24 Hour City initiatives adopted by local authorities include licensing initiatives, such as staggering closing times to avoid concentrations of people and increasing the number of late-night licences; bridging the gap between offices closing and the start of entertainment activities through, for example, shops closing later; the stimulation of cafe and restaurant activity; the promotion of street entertainment and festivals.

Mixed use

Ever since Jane Jacobs published her landmark polemical essay in 1961, there has been support for mixed occupancy and use of urban areas, in contrast to a planning orthodoxy in the post-war years that had encouraged segregation and zoning. More recently, problematic domination of certain public spaces by monocultures (for example young drinkers in town centres at night) has highlighted the importance of achieving a more balanced and varied use of public space. 'Living over the shop' has been an increasingly favoured approach to get more people back into British town centres; this was pioneered in Norwich and is now increasingly part of planning policy throughout the country. City-centre residents add extra informal surveillance to public spaces and, as they have a vested interest in the neighbourhood, are more likely to report or act on problems.

Inclusive designs

Most of these interventions don't seem to have much to do with design, but even things like CCTV need good design (to allow clear lines of sight), security personnel don't want hidden corners and entrapment spots, and managers and animators need physical facilities and spaces in which to organize services and activities. All this points to an *indirect* role for good urban design. However, some commentators suggest that the way we design or redesign streets and public spaces can *directly* contribute to their sociable and law-abiding use by all citizens (Billingham and Cole 2002, CABE 2004a and b, Gehl 2003).

Accommodating deviance and unpredictability

Efforts to sanitize and control every inch of public space risk that we eliminate all the 'shadowed' (Wood 1981) or 'slack' (Worpole and Knox 2007) places that allow for activities that the participants don't want to be seen or heard by others. Clearly, some of these deviant activities will be illegal and intolerable, but as Denis Wood persuasively argues, if we clear these screened places, we also remove the possibilities of deviant activities that are harmless or positively valuable as articulations of resistance to the status quo: 'it would be a dead world indeed without the shadowed spaces' (Wood p95). Worpole and Knox also argue that 'Slack spaces are needed (or should be acknowledged where they already exist) where minor infringements of local by-laws, such as skateboarding, den-building, informal ball games, hanging out and drinking, are regulated with a light touch' (Worpole and

Figure 18 Fort Worth, Texas

Knox 2007 p14). Depending on one's degree of tolerance one could also add to this list (as does Denis Wood): nose-picking, heavy petting, premarital or extramarital sex and nude swimming. Worpole and Knox point out that citizens are very good at self-regulation and that this is the best way to handle such grey areas. It is also important to remember that in a democratic and civilized society, homeless people, alcoholics, those receiving 'care in the community' and 'tribes' of young people are citizens just like anyone else and

therefore should be allowed to occupy public space, so long as their presence is not causing a real threat to the safety of others. In fact, such marginalized groups are usually very good at finding their own 'slack' or shadowed spaces where they can get on with their own lives out the way of others.

Figure 19 Bristol

Figure 20
Torquay, Devon

Caroline Holland and her fellow researchers, who studied social interactions in public spaces in Aylesbury, England (2007), concluded that: 'The vitality of the urban scene requires some degree of human unpredictability. Indeed it is often the offer of chaos, chance or coincidence that makes many want to celebrate the potential of public space' (Findings summary p4).

Examples of this might be children who play with the flooring materials and puddles in playgrounds (rather than the swings and climbing frames); stunt bikers who make use of walls and different levels in plazas; or language exchange students who colonize a particular city-centre space as a meeting place.

Figure 21
Krakow, Poland

Some lessons from two case studies

Birmingham

The shopping mall built above Birmingham's main railway station is a curious hybrid of public/private space. It is used as a pedestrian route into and out of the subterranean station platforms and, as with many such central locations, was a warm and covered gathering spot for people with nowhere else to go (and not necessarily any money to spend). The centre management responded to this by removing the communal seating, so that there is now no other reason to be there other than to shop or purchase refreshments in a cafe (Figure 22).

There is some limited communal seating in the Convention Quarter, part of Birmingham's mixed use inner-city revitalization but, in an even more draconian response than that at the shopping mall above the station, unauthorized users are completely excluded from the residential areas by access-controlled gates. The developers and property managers would undoubtedly justify this extreme version of exclusion by asserting that it was the best way to attract higher-income residents back into the inner city, but it does mean that substantial tracts of open space in central Birmingham are inaccessible to ordinary citizens.

Figure 22 Seatless shopping mall, Birmingham

Figure 23 Birmingham Convention Quarter residential area

Toronto

As mentioned earlier, shopping malls have, in some ways, become the new version of the 'village pump', where citizens gather in all weathers to use services but also to mingle with others and possibly socialize. The trouble is that, because malls are privately owned, what the public is allowed to do or not to do is at the whim and under the control of the landlords. Unlike real public spaces, the primary purpose of a shopping mall is to generate profits for the businesses that operate there. This does not inevitably lead to the exclusion of 'non-consumption' activities, but usually they will have to be justified in terms of business benefits. Two very different approaches to this have been taken in shopping malls in Toronto, as described below.

An exclusionary approach to people management was taken at the Eaton Centre, the huge mall that dominates the centre of Toronto. The Centre had a large team of security guards who among other things were tasked with enforcing the exclusion of several thousand Toronto residents who were deemed to be 'undesirable' (presumably the homeless, alcoholics, drug addicts and problematic young people) (Poole 1994). It may or may not have been a coincidence that the mall's owners filed for bankruptcy in 1999 and were taken over by the Sears group.

By way of complete contrast, only a few miles to the west, the management of the Dufferin Mall adopted a completely different approach. Set in one of Toronto's less salubrious but most cosmopolitan neighbourhoods, Dufferin Mall is the main local retail centre and thus attracts a cross-section of the local population. In the early 1990s, the Mall was experiencing serious crime problems, as a result of theft and violent and threatening behaviour by gangs

Figure 24 Dufferin Mall food court, Toronto

of young people who were using the Mall, and particularly the food court, as a place to 'hang out'. Many local people, particularly women, were avoiding the Mall because they regarded it as a dangerous place. Rather than filtering out all those but serious shoppers, the management of Dufferin Mall made a conscious and successful effort to engage socially as well as commercially with all its users and the surrounding community. Their philosophy, as explained by David Hall, the manager at the time of these changes, is that 'The better the quality of neighbourhood life, the better the business environment – a reciprocal relationship placing an onus on business to assume its full share of responsibility for ameliorating social problems – business giving back to the community that supports it.' The practical outcome of this commitment was a huge range of integrative and involving activities centred on the Mall, including a community newspaper, youth work, play facilities, a literacy programme, educational outreach work with school truants and excludees and drop-in centres in some shop units for different advice and counselling services. The Mall achieved significant reductions in crime and disorder – a 38 per cent drop in reported crime over a five-year period (Wekerle 1999), and is now hugely popular with local people, showing the sound commercial sense of such an inclusive approach to the whole population.

For a more detailed account of the Dufferin Mall social intervention programme go to: www.phac-aspc.gc.ca/ph-sp/phdd/implement/dufferin-mall-story.html

Summary

As with so many areas of study that involve real people in real environments, it is difficult to untangle the various strands (covered earlier) that might influence human behaviour either for better or worse in public spaces. Given the complexity and adaptabiliy of the human species it would be far too simplistic to say that the way we design the urban realm has a *direct* influence on how *everyone* will behave in it, apart from such things as impregnable physical barriers. It seems more likely that design and physical layout will have a softer type of influence that will interact with other factors such as location, management, 'animation' and culture. Layered on top of all this complex series of interactions is the whole political frame of social aspiration, i.e. what kind of society do we want? To complicate matters still further, we may say we want one thing (say 'an urban renaissance') yet our desire for other things (such as 'security' and 'control') may actually lead to practices that achieve the latter and deny us the former.

There appear to be two issues that transcend the 'designing out crime versus designing in good behaviour' debate. First, there is the important business of community control, which seems to be one of the most important differentiators between safe and unsafe neighbourhoods. Generally one can say that the more community control and social cohesion there is in a neighbourhood, the safer that neighbourhood is. See for example Hirschfield and Bowers 1997, Sampson et al

Figure 25 Backwell, Somerset

1997. Interestingly, both sides of the safer environments debate claim that their methods generate informal social control, but through different means and on a different scale. Supporters of gated communities (see Figure 25) would argue that such neighbourhoods encourage social cohesion and on the other hand, many new urbanist developments (particularly in the US) have turned out to be quite exclusive (for example 'Seaside' and 'Celebration' in Florida).

Second, and most importantly, we need to decide what quality of urban life we want. Do we want a mostly privatized existence, centred on our well-defended homes and exclusive clubs, where we interact only with a few like-minded friends and colleagues? In which case we should go for 'defended space'. Or do we want a more open quality of life in which we can wander where we please, encounter lots of different people, but take a few more risks in the process? In theory, 'new urbanism' delivers this more zestful way of life but, as Town and O'Toole's article points out, many new urbanism developments are turning out to be monocultural and riddled with regulations. So it may be that neither defensible space nor new urbanism can provide us with the kind of vibrant neighbourhoods that could be stimulating to live and work in. Maybe we should adopt policies and practices in regeneration that both adopt reasonable levels of security and encourage designs that allow for interaction and integration, as traditional small towns did throughout history!

Ultimately, levels of crime and safety are more likely to be determined by bigger socio-economic, cultural, socialization and geographical factors than they are by the design of our urban spaces, which takes us back to the original two images in this chapter.

Finally, however, I wouldn't want to suggest that the built environment is irrelevant as a *backdrop* to human behaviour. I believe that architects, planners and urban designers have an important role to play in designing or redesigning safe and secure neighbourhoods, but their contribution is part of a much bigger whole.

Children and Public Space

Outdoor space is hugely important for children's development (Moore 1986). It is important for their health, both mental and physical, and is potentially one of the most exciting places for them to play. I say *potentially* because we often provide them with stultifying environments which offer very little delight, adventure or scope for them to exercise their imaginations (see Figures 26 and 27).

Healthy outdoor play has been emasculated in many areas by adult preoccupations with health and safety, potential litigation, stranger danger, poor maintenance, economies in public services and even aesthetics. Despite various media-fuelled panics, children are in no more danger in public spaces than 30 years ago (see Goodchild and Owen 2007). In fact, as some commentators have noted, as mollycoddling parents keep their kids indoors and local authorities remove any trace of adventurous opportunities from the public realm, children are more likely to die of boredom than from any outdoor public danger.

The general trend for outdoor play provision in the UK for the last 50 years has been to provide robust fixed equipment in fenced-off designated areas (usually in a corner of a recreation field).

Figure 26 Charente Maritime, France

Figure 27 Dornoch, Scotland

Undoubtedly, some of these 'ghettos of swings and springy chickens' have been reasonably successful, but even a cursory observation of the multitude of these spaces scattered around our towns and villages will reveal underuse if not abandonment. However, a different approach in parts of continental Europe, now being gradually incorporated in the UK (following the lead of Stirling in Scotland), is resulting in more vibrant play provision for children. Three features of this different approach are integration into the townscape, mixed use and loose materials.

Figure 28 Backwell, Somerset

Figure 29 Paris

Integration into the townscape

Children and their accompanying carers prefer short journeys to play areas and therefore it is likely that spaces will be better used if they are part of the neighbourhood. This can also create livelier places for all.

The example in Krakow (Figure 30) benefits both parents and children, as well as creating a lively scene for passers-by.

In the Amsterdam example (Figure 31), part of the street has been reclaimed as a dedicated play space, with only emergency or special access being allowed for vehicles.

Mixed use

The Krakow example also highlights the value of having facilities for adults as well as children. This will usually consist of seating with a cafe or picnic tables (Figures 32 and 33).

Figure 30 Krakow, Poland

Figure 31 Amsterdam

Figure 32 Radstock, Somerset

Figure 33 Copenhagen

Loose materials

When they have the choice, children are more inclined to play with natural elements, such as water, sand and wood. This seems to allow them to be much more creative, which, after all, should be a valuable outcome of play.

In Germany (most notably in Freiburg and Berlin) play-space providers have wholeheartedly embraced this looser, more naturalistic approach, with the resulting playgrounds looking very different from the shiny metal and rubber-matted surfaces that characterize many British playgrounds.

In Edinburgh, a new play area created in the inner-city green space known as 'The Meadows' (Figure 36 overleaf) has combined the more traditional fixed play attractions with copious quantities of sand, wood bark chippings and water channels. The play space has proved to be hugely popular with children, adolescents and their parents.

Figure 34 Combe Dingle, Bristol

Figure 35 Gropiusstadt, Berlin

Figure 36 Play space, The Meadows, Edinburgh

Risk and adventure

As mentioned previously, many play and recreation areas in the UK have become increasingly sterile and useless as a result of adult and statutory authorities' fears about safety. There is an increasing recognition that this 'risk-averse' culture has gone too far and indeed both the British Health and Safety Executive (HSE) and the Royal Society for the Prevention of Accidents (RoSPA) have issued guidance to play providers that a reasonable amount of risk in play is perfectly acceptable as long as the benefits outweigh the risks. The main inhibitors to more adventurous play for our children remain parents, along with local authority lawyers and insurance companies.

Unpredictable use

It has been noted by some play experts that children will often get the most out of play facilities when they use what is there in ways other than intended. This should be encouraged, or at least be allowed for, as it can lead to more creativity. An example

Figure 37 Central Bristol

might be children playing with the sand or loose bark that has been provided as a soft surface material. Furthermore, children will seize play opportunities even in environments that are not explicitly designated as play spaces. This may be one way to partly get round the legal liability dilemma that some local authorities fear – designate a public structure as art or a water feature, rather than as a playful space.

This leads to a further point – some of the most exciting spaces for children and young people to play in are shadowy or spare bits of the urban fabric: patches of wasteland where you can make 'dens', banks of streams and rivers where you can get muddy. As we gradually clean up and control every nook and cranny of the urban realm, we are in danger of losing such 'loose' places.

Figure 38 Hanging out and skating, Barcelona

Addressing the Use of Public Space by Young People

The segment of the population most likely to be found in, and to benefit from, public space is young people. Yet, for adults at least, the presence of some young people, particularly teenagers, in public spaces is seen as most demanding and potentially problematic. Young people and particularly adolescents are at a very vulnerable and influential developmental stage in their lives. What happens to them during these transitional years will influence their long-term physical and mental health. Repressing their natural inclinations to get out of their homes and learn to playfully socialize risks displacing their energies into the very things that concerned parents are trying to avoid – drug misuse, self-harm and delinquency. It is ironic that parents who are trying to protect their children by not allowing them to go out and play or socialize on their own may in many cases be doing more harm than good. They may be able to temporarily repress their offsprings' inclination to engage in risky, antisocial or illegal outdoor activity, but, in so doing, they may turn them into unhealthy 'bedroom recluses', cramping both their physical and psychological development in the process.

In the United Kingdom we mostly dislike young people. We call them derogatory names (e.g. yobbos, vandals, thugs, tearaways)

Figure 39 Hanging out in York

that we wouldn't dare use for any other segment of the population. They are often seen as being 'guilty before proven innocent', as in the case of 'threatening gangs of youths' gathering in public spaces.

The standard strategic response to groups of young people in public or communal areas is to try to force them out – either by moving them on (using police, security guards or CCTV), threatening them with penalties (e.g. fines for skateboarding), or removing the opportunities for them to gather at all (e.g. the removal of seating in public spaces where young people have started to hang out).

But the phenomenon of young people socializing in groups away from immediate adult supervision is an important developmental stage – moving from the family nest to independent adulthood (Waiton 2001). We should be enabling this healthy socialization process by ensuring that there are places and spaces where youngsters can gather and 'hang out'. And young people don't want to be shunted into the margins of neighbourhoods – they usually and rightly demand equal access to the prime sites such as town centres, parks, high streets and malls.

Young people gather in what are seen by adults as inappropriate places because we do not provide *appropriate* places. Where are they meant to gather? Homes have got smaller. Youth clubs have been cut back. Members of the public call the police if youths gather at bus shelters, in alleyways or outside shops at night.

Adults often worry that if teenagers are allowed to gather with minimum supervision and surveillance, they will engage in risky and illegal activities. This is used as a justification to move young people on, impose curfews and ban them from specific locations using sanctions such as dispersal orders. It is true that they will sometimes make fools of themselves, take a few risks, get too boisterous and show off in front of their peers. However, it is better to let them do these things in designated spaces out of harm's way, than to try and repress such activities altogether. At best this merely moves the problem and it may well lead to other more serious difficulties that could cost dearly in the long term. We can't stop kids indulging in sex, drugs and rock'n'roll; indeed the more we try to ban these, the more attractive they appear to rebellious youth determined to kick against the traces of adult censure. We therefore need to take

harm reduction and risk management approaches to such activities, to minimize potential damage both to young people and the adults affected by them.

Fortunately, not all our strategies for the use of spaces by young people are aimed at excluding them. Some imaginative solutions to the need for young people to gather and 'hang out' include:

- **Youth shelters and sports systems.** These consist of good quality structures where young people can gather without supervision and without causing annoyance to adult residents (see Hampshire and Wilkinson 2002). Some shelters have been designed and even built by the target group of young people themselves. If young people have been involved in this or in other ways, they are more likely to safeguard 'their' investment.

Figure 40 Youth shelter, Hayle Cornwall

Figure 41 Ciaia Park, Wrexham

The location of such shelters is critical – not so close to homes that adults become irritated, but not so isolated that young people are vulnerable to uncontrolled victimization. It is also important that they are regularly maintained, as if successful they are likely to experience a lot of wear and tear.

■ **Adventure playgrounds.** Sadly, these rough, tough and tumble locations have mostly been emasculated by health and safety worries, with the result that many young people have fewer opportunities to experiment and take risks under benign adult supervision. Enterprising as

they are, some young people have discovered that the entire urban realm is a potential adventure playground and, from its start in France, the *parcours* or 'free-running' movement has burgeoned in many cities. This involves the use of walls and other built features as daring structures to jump over, between or from – a beautiful example of subverting the original intentions of the built environment to create a healthy (if dangerous and potentially illegal) activity. A few proper adventure playgrounds do survive, including an inspiring one in the middle of Ciaia Park, Wrexham – the largest housing estate in North Wales.

■ **Skateboarding, stunt bike and rollerblading spaces.** Such spaces work best when young people have been involved in their design and location. An inspiring example can be found in central Brussels, where a site over the main railway line that cuts through the centre has been made into an urban space for all, with a built-in skateboarding bowl, designed according to the specification of a group of local skaters. The space works as an attraction for young and old alike.

Design and management implications

We need to 'design in' the facilities and locations where children and young people can meet, play and socialize in reasonable safety, but without totally removing the excitement and 'buzz' that young people need. On the other hand we must minimize the danger and victimization that young people all too often experience in public spaces (Percy-Smith and Matthews 2001). Finding this balance between adventure and mollycoddling requires an approach that includes design, management and social interventions.

One of the most important strategies is to include young people themselves in the planning, design and management of public spaces (White 1998). Grown-ups don't necessarily know best and even if they think they do, the *process* of involvement is as important as the physical outcome. For example, where young people have been involved in the choice and construction of youth shelters, there have been fewer subsequent problems with their use and maintenance (Hampshire and Wilkinson 2002).

We should remind ourselves that young people are citizens just as much as adults are; indeed they represent society's future. If you ask young people, they will tell you what they want and they will often be keen to get involved in providing services and facilities. It has been said that: 'Young people these days – they'll take anything, especially responsibility.'

Figure 42 Central Brussels, Belgium

Young people are likely to want both structured and unstructured facilities and activities. Different groups and individuals will want different things. One size does not fit all (White 1998). You cannot just provide one skateboard ramp and assume you have fulfilled your obligations to youth. Young people want to hang out with their own particular clique or gang. Fourteen-year-olds will not necessarily want to be in the same places as 12-year-olds – a couple of years make a huge difference at that age. If you just provide one facility without providing for adaptable use or dedicated locations for other groups, you may find that there is conflict over space and the intended target group is edged out.

Location and journey time to facilities for young people are crucial factors. Generally speaking, facilities for pre-teens need to be very close to where they live and need to be closely managed by adults or, in the case of open play spaces, they need to be visible from parents' homes. Pocket parks in squares or closes surrounded by housing are safer and likely to be better used than play spaces in the corner of more distant parks and open spaces. By contrast, teenagers prefer locations with lower supervision that are not immediately overlooked by parents' homes. However they don't want to be completely isolated from the general public. Teenagers are concerned for their own safety and rightly so – they are at particularly high risk of being victimized (National Centre for Social Research 1998). However, despite the prevailing moral panic about 'stranger danger', it should be pointed out that children and young people are much more likely to be victims at the hands of their peers and family than they are by adult strangers. Concerned parents who won't let their children go out on their own for fear that they might be abducted by paedophiles and psychopaths, while minimizing one statistically low risk, increase the risk of cramping the healthy and social development of their offspring.

Figure 43 Harlem, New York. Because there is nowhere else for them to meet, these young men in Harlem have colonized the area that had been designed for parents to sit in while they kept an eye on their children in the adjacent playground.

Although dedicated locations sometimes work, young people should be entitled to equal rights of access to general public space. As part of their development it is valuable that they learn to interact with other citizens. Adults can provide informal social control and supervision and can call on specialist agencies if problems arise. Young people probably feel safer in areas that are also accessible to adults, such as town squares, public car parks, footpaths and parks.

Planners and urban designers may feel deeply frustrated when the area they designed as an outdoor seating area for office workers becomes colonized by skateboarders (Figure 44). But is this a disaster, or should we regard public spaces as dynamic, organic and adaptable, rather than for a fixed single use? (Sennett 1973).

Figure 44 Central Cardiff

Conclusion

In the UK we mostly regard young people as potential problems, preferably to be excluded from public space. This repressive approach damages young people's potential for healthy, prosocial development, and means that they resort to more devious means to 'hang out', or even more worryingly, become neurotic bedroom recluses.

We need to respond positively, inclusively and creatively to the needs of young people to socialize in public spaces by involving them in design and provision, and ensuring that what is provided minimizes harm and victimization risk, without removing the *frisson* that young people need and enjoy.

CHAPTER THREE

What Makes a Space Convivial?

Principles and Underpinnings

As a bridge between theory and practice, there are various aspects of the design and management of public spaces that affect how successful or problematic they may be. This section covers some of these 'principles and underpinnings'.

A number of people have attempted to establish a set of 'principles' to inform the design and production of successful urban spaces. Francis Tibbalds (1989 p467), for example, suggested the following 'Ten Commandments' of urban design, most of which are directly applicable to public spaces:

1   *Thou shalt consider places before buildings*
2   *Thou shalt have the humility to learn from the past and respect the context of buildings and sites*
3   *Thou shalt encourage the mixing of uses in towns and cities*
4   *Thou shalt design on a human scale*
5   *Thou shalt encourage the freedom to walk about*
6   *Thou shalt cater for all sections of the community and consult with them*
7   *Thou shalt build legible environments*
8   *Thou shalt build to last and adapt*
9   *Thou shalt avoid change on too great a scale at any one time*
10 *Thou shalt, with all the means available, promote intricacy, joy and visual delight in the built environment.*

These principles are closely aligned to the urban design values espoused by Jacobs and Appleyard (1987) in their 'urban design manifesto'. This was a reaction to the modernist and mechanistic approach that had been promoted by the Congrès International d'Architecture Moderne (CIAM) in its famous *Athens Charter* of 1933, published in heavily edited form by Le Corbusier and colleagues in 1943.

Mixed use and new types of urbanism

After the Second World War planning in Europe and North America was heavily influenced by the thinking of the CIAM and favoured a 'zoning' approach, where different types of uses were allocated to different areas of the city; so that all industry was in one place, residential in another and leisure facilities in yet another, and so on. This was found, over time, to create a number of adverse side effects and, in relation to the subject of this book, it often resulted in the abandonment of central public areas for significant times of day or days of the week, as well as creating bland and indeterminate open spaces around residential blocks. As a reaction to this, there emerged the 'urban villages' movement in the UK (see Neal 2003) and 'new urbanism' in the US (see Duany and Plater-Zyberk 1991). The fundamental idea underpinning this approach is to mix uses together to create more integrated neighbourhoods, which are more sustainable and capable of building 'social capital', as people are more likely to know each other and interact. Public spaces are a core part of this new urbanist or urban village approach. By providing more 'eyes on the street' and community cohesion, these new developments (or reworking of old ones) are also supposed to be safer and more resistant to crime and antisocial behaviour. However, they have come under some criticism (see for example Town and O'Toole 2005) and some of the brand new flagship developments, such as Poundbury in England and Seaside in Florida, US, have turned out to be worryingly monocultural with underused public space. Other more low-key developments that are better integrated into the surrounding urban fabric (such as Bordesley urban village in Birmingham) seem to work better.

Legibility

This is a term originally coined, for urban design purposes, by Kevin Lynch (1960). He defines it as 'the ease with which [the cityscape's] parts can be recognised and can be organised into a coherent pattern' (p2). So, in terms of public space, it means

Figure 45 Poundbury, Dorset

knowing where you are, knowing how to get to where you want to be and feeling that the space has visual coherence. Yet, as a result of accretions of street furniture and signs, many of our public spaces are incoherent and confusing.

The problem of unacceptable stuff in the public realm can be categorized under seven headings:

1   **Clutter** – general uncoordinated street equipment, signs and furniture.

Figure 46 Clifton, Bristol

2   **Confusion and contradiction** (including misdirection by signs that have been knocked or turned in the wrong direction).

3   **Duplication of equipment**

Figure 47 Castle Park, Bristol

4   **Illegibility** (literally) – signs that you can't read because they have not been cleaned or maintained, or are obscured by vegetation.
5   **Interruptions and obstructions** – such as having waste bins, lamp posts, bike racks and so on, located in the middle of footpaths.
6   **Redundancy** – old equipment or fittings that have not been removed.
7   **Uncoordination** – different things added by different departments or agencies, with no overall consistency of design or integration.

Figure 48 Harbourside, Bristol

The environmental psychologists Rachel and Stephen Kaplan assert that the coherence and legibility of the public realm is important, as 'the struggle to pay attention in cluttered and confusing environments turns out to be central to what is experienced as mental fatigue' (Kaplan and Kaplan 1989 p182).

Firmness or looseness?

In the UK in particular, the whole system from planning through to detailed design and construction allows for very little flexibility – the very thing that the evolution of convivial spaces requires. The result is that we too often end up with rigid designs that cannot easily be changed, once it is found they are not well adjusted for optimum use. A looser 'see what happens' approach with money held back for adjustments and modifications is likely to deliver spaces much more attuned to user needs (see Brand 1994). As Andersson (2002) observes: '… the design of a city must be regarded as an ongoing process, one that people need time to become acquainted with' (p112). He goes on to give the example of Sergels Torg, a plaza in central Stockholm which was built with stark modernist zeal in the early 1970s, but soon declined into desolation and misuse. Modest, incremental changes begun in 1998 (such as lighting, resurfacing and changed circulation arrangements) have helped to make it a more successful gathering place, as originally intended, although its fundamental design as a sunken, hard space surrounded by traffic means that it will never be entirely 'convivial'.

Figure 49 Sergels Torg, Stockholm

Attempts to establish principles for what makes a successful public space, will be influenced by the values of the person defining them and are thus 'normative' (to use the social science jargon). However, there are some more objective underpinnings that can inform good design and management, based on the nature of human behaviour and preference, many of which have been clarified with the help of environmental psychology.

The Psychology of Public Space

Public spaces serve a number of practical functions, being places for trading, meeting, conversing, resting and so on. Yet there is an additional dimension to public space – it can fulfil certain psychological needs as well as purely physical ones. By 'psychology' in this context, I mean anything that affects our behaviour or feelings.

There has been substantial interest and study over the years into the relationship between human behaviour and urban form (see for example Canter 1974, 1977, Rapoport 1977, 1990, plus the journals *Environment and Behaviour* and *Journal of Environmental Psychology*). In some fields, most notably urban security, this has had a substantial influence on the design and management of urban spaces. An extreme position in this respect is the 'design determinist' one, where theoreticians such as Alice Coleman (1985) blamed badly designed built environments for 'causing' the high levels of crime being

committed in them. At the other end of this continuum of thinking about the degree to which design of space can influence behaviour are those who note the degree to which people can adapt to their surroundings and 'make the best of a bad job'. In truth it is likely that we both affect and are affectd by space. In terms of designing good public spaces, it helps to understand how people are likely to respond and relate to the space available and how they make spaces work for them. Some of this will relate to some basic human behavioural characteristics such as territoriality, interpersonal distance, distribution and the need for different types of observation and communication (Canter 1974). Other responses are to do with such psychological effects as interpretation, coherence, legibility, sense of safety, intrigue and curiosity.

Territoriality

One of the most fundamental human traits (presumably from our tribal hunter-gatherer origins) is the need to mark and claim territory. This is potentially problematic in public open space, because in theory it belongs to everyone and no one. In extreme cases public spaces will be colonized by certain groups, perhaps youth gangs or street drinkers, but more often there is a kind of accommodation between various groups and interests, which at best makes for lively, varied and intriguing occupation of space, allowing people to observe diversity and difference without having to get directly involved in it.

Figure 50 Padua

Interpersonal distance

Linked to the above points about territoriality is the need to keep appropriate distance or proximity according to relationship. In the photo above, taken in Padua, the couple intertwined in the foreground contrast with the strangers from another culture surrounding them, who are trying to distance themselves in a tight situation by turning away. If there is choice of sitting and lingering places and some are unoccupied, it is normal to sit on or occupy a vacant space some distance away from the others already there, rather than sitting right next to a stranger. Indeed people who sit right next to strangers, when there is opportunity to do otherwise, are treated with suspicion and discomfort by those already occupying the space. As the space becomes more congested, people have to accommodate themselves gradually more closely to each other, but always according to some unwritten law about 'reasonable distance'.

Distribution

However, it has been noted (see for example Canter 1974, Whyte 1980) that people do not distribute themselves evenly across an entire public space. There are certain preferred locations where people tend to cluster and others that people try to avoid. Generally, locations where one can observe others without being exposed from all sides oneself are preferred. This may explain the enduring attraction of ledges (where one's back is protected by the wall behind) and the avoidance of backless benches in the centre of public spaces (unless there is no other choice).

The need for different types of observation and communication

Interpersonal distance will be determined (if there is any choice) by the activities people are engaged in, in public space. People who are only there 'to watch the world go by' will want to be further away from others than those who are hoping to have some kind of casual interaction, who in turn would be further away than those who are interacting with close friends. A good public space will offer the chance for the whole range of these activities to occur and this has implications for the arrangement of places to sit or linger. If the space consists of an area of closely cut grass then this range is easily accommodated (Figure 52), but if the area is hard landscaped then careful consideration will have to be given to the location of benches, as well as informal seating and leaning opportunities such as ledges, steps and low walls. The ideal is movable seating (see page 102), but this is not always practicable.

Figure 51 Harbourside, Bristol

Figure 52 College Green, Bristol

Interpretation, legibility and coherence

Our minds are skilled at 'reading' space – i.e. identifying where we are and the qualities it appears to offer. Again, this is probably an inheritance from our ancestors who had to identify and memorize suitable hunting and gathering grounds. This is mostly done through visual interpretation of the cues a space gives us, both in terms of its built form and the kind of activities (or *lack* of activities) going on there. A fair amount of research has been done into how we extract 'meaning' from space (see for example Canter 1977, Rapoport 1977, Madanipour 1996). For Kevin Lynch (1960) a good place

should be 'legible', by which he means '... the ease with which its parts can be recognised and can be organised into a coherent pattern' (p2). How this coherence is achieved is the subject of some debate in urban design circles. In theory a coherent space should be all of a piece, yet many of the spaces that people love contain variety and diversity, both of built form and activity.

Sense of safety

One of the things that people are adept at 'reading' (if not always accurately so) is the degree to which an unfamiliar place appears to be safe or unsafe. This is a crucial factor that will significantly determine whether or not they choose to linger in that space. They will gauge how safe a place appears to be (in terms of risk of personal victimization) by studying the people occupying that space, but also by looking at physical attributes (such as the amount of light, potential hiding places and entrapment spots). The assessment of risk will depend on who you are – generally people will feel more at ease when they see people similar to them already occupying that space in a relaxed way. This has particular implications for the facilities and management of public space, as there is a risk that certain demographic groups (such as older people, women, disabled people and those from ethnic minorities) will feel nervous about using certain public spaces, even if their risk of victimization is quite low (see Shaftoe 2004). The design of public spaces should also allow for clear views and the possibility of easy escape or refuge.

Intrigue and curiosity

People want coherence and a sense of safety in public spaces, but they don't want blandness (Kaplan and Kaplan 1989, Marsh 1990). One of the psychological attractions of a good public space is the promise that it will satisfy our innate curiosity. We like to be intrigued by the possibility that there is more to a space than initially meets the eye and that if we move through it there may be further intriguing discoveries. This underpins the attraction of unfolding townscapes as espoused by Cullen (1961), where a series of linked but not immediately visible spaces are designed to gradually reveal themselves as you move through them. This is also an important factor in good park design – there is nothing more boring than a park or green space where you can immediately see everything that is there.

Aesthetics

Woven into all this psychology of space are our aesthetic experiences, which are discussed in the next section.

Figure 53 Bland green space, Dublin

Aesthetics – Sensing the Character of an Area

Constricted, we understand and interpret the city through the technical rather than the sensory, yet it is the sensory from which we build feeling and emotion and through which our personal psychological landscapes are built. These in turn determine how well or badly a place works – even economically, let alone socially or culturally – and how it feels to its inhabitants and visitors. (Landry 2006 p40)

Sensuous requirements may coincide or conflict with other demands but cannot be separated from them in designing or judging, nor are they 'impractical' or merely decorative, or even nobler than other concerns. Sensing is indispensable to being alive. (Lynch 1971 p189)

As Westerners, we all spend most of our time in the *built* environment. If we are not in buildings, we are surrounded by them when we go out. If we are not surrounded by buildings – in the countryside – we are still surrounded by people-made structures: walls, roads, paths, terracing, ponds, sea defences and so on. Nearly all these built items have a function and can therefore be regarded as existing for technical reasons – the house to keep us warm and dry, the stone wall to protect the crops, the road to get us from one place to another easily. It can be argued that even structures that are not obviously functional, such as monuments, do actually serve a functional purpose, such as marking a location or asserting power. However, as the quotations opening this section highlight, in addition to all this technical function, places and spaces affect us aesthetically – they affect our minds and senses. This is not just a trivial spin-off from their true technical purpose, for by affecting our minds and senses these spaces and places can profoundly influence our health and wellbeing, for better or worse. (See for example Appleyard 1981, Halpern 1995, Guite et al 2006.) As Thomsen (1998) remarks, when talking about the *ambiance* of cities: 'Architecture without sense appeal makes people moody, grumpy, at first emotionally unsatisfied and then physically ill' (p103).

Figure 54 Eastville Park, Bristol

Kaplan and Kaplan point out in their book *The Experience of Nature* (1989) that: 'Aesthetic reactions reflect neither a casual nor a trivial aspect of the human makeup. Rather, they appear to constitute a guide to human behaviour that is both ancient and far-reaching. Underlying such reactions is an assessment of the environment in terms of its compatibility with human needs and purposes. Thus aesthetic reaction is an indication of an environment where effective human functioning is likely to occur' (p10).

This section will analyse the visual and non-visual aesthetic qualities of successful public spaces in an attempt to arrive at some broader aesthetic principles. There will be some emphasis on the non-visual senses, as urban design has, in the past, underplayed these, preferring instead to concentrate almost exclusively on the look of places.

Figure 55 Zaragoza, Spain

Despite the latter point, the *visual* impression of place is likely to be the most powerful sensory experience for people with good sight. Furthermore, as Landry (2006) reminds us 'sights are better articulated, because in general we have a rich vocabulary around physical appearance' (p50). Not only can we describe visual qualities with words, but we can augment them with maps, plans, drawings and photographs. But as Rasmussen (1959) notes: 'It is not enough to see architecture; you must experience it' (p33).

Although it could be argued that the main aesthetic experience of most public spaces is a visual one, they affect the senses in other ways, most noticeably aurally. The sounds (mostly traffic) of the big city penetrate all but the most secluded of urban spaces. Where there are water features, lakes, harbours or rivers, weirs and fountains produce relatively high levels of white noise in contrast to the silence of still water.

Figure 56 Frome Valley, Bristol

The other sense that is noticeably affected, even in urban spaces, is the feeling of warmth or coolness caused by the microclimate. Variations in shelter and shade can affect wind chill and the degree to which the warmth of the sun can penetrate.

In terms of smell, the usual urban pollutants (such as exhaust fumes) are likely to be noticeable and it may be that at certain times of the year the smell of vegetation (either flourishing or decaying) could be a significant sensory factor. However, it could also be the *absence* of smell that could make somewhere an aesthetically pleasing environment, as in cities we can be overwhelmed by too much olfactory stimulation.

Finally, urban spaces can have some noticeable textural qualities, both in terms of the different types of surfacing underfoot and the qualities of built features and foliage, which, even if not actually touched, can be experienced.

If our understanding is limited to a visual understanding, we only concentrate on shapes. If, however, we go beyond appearances, we start a spatial understanding, a three dimensional experience. We can enter this space, rather than just see it. The same applies to the design of spaces. We do not create mere appearances but spaces that we can use for different purposes. (Madanipour 1996 p99)

Figure 57 Parc Guell, Barcelona – powerfully textural

Movement

As mentioned by Taylor (2008), movement through space (along with time of day and seasons) has to be factored into any consideration of aesthetic principles, and this applies just as much to non-visual as visual aspects. Unless we are sitting, lingering or

loitering, we generally experience the environment as we move between places. In relation to non-visual aesthetic experience this will include the feeling of surfaces underfoot, the air or wind against our skin, and the effort of passing through a space, particularly if this entails climbing or descending. All these factors should therefore be considered as part of the urban design of a space, and assuming we want people to have *positive* aesthetic experiences (Taylor 2008) we should optimize surface treatments, microclimates and gradients to provide the best sensory experiences.

The photograph of a stepped path leading up to an urban park in Bristol (Figure 58) encapsulates some of these points. The paving is smooth but uneven, giving it a tactile effect, even when wearing sturdy shoes. As Lennard and Lennard (1995 p38) point out:

This type of thoughtfully constructed floorscape can also be a work of art that increases the pedestrian's enjoyment and awareness of the experience of walking. Each step is special and unique, and the effect, as in a Zen garden, is to focus attention on the present moment, the immediate sensory experience, the feel of the paving underfoot, the changing materials. ... This intensification of one's awareness of 'being here', in a pleasing environment intensifies one's sense of wellbeing.

Figure 58 Eastville Park, Bristol

The relatively gentle slope of the stepped path also demonstrates the importance of handling gradients appropriately. Clearly the topography of the site will be the fundamental determinant of levels and inclines, but it appears that, as long as the changes are not too steep, people enjoy the three-dimensionality created by slopes and tiers (for example the popularity of the sloping Piazza Del Campo in Siena and the Spanish Steps in Rome). Changes in level will inevitably be *felt* by the pedestrian (through differential physical exertion), as well as *seen*. However, it should also be noted that, in dense urban spaces, people prefer to be at street level rather than on raised decks or sunken plazas (see the research of Whyte 1980 and Gehl 2003).

Finally, the microclimate, which affects our feeling of warmth or coolness can be considerately designed through the use of enclosure versus exposure and planting. Generally in Northern Europe we need to protect people from the wind and cold and maximize access to daylight, whereas in other, hotter parts of the world, spaces might be designed to encourage cooling breezes to pass through and to provide shade from the baking sun. As well as using walls and buildings to create a protective microclimate, shrubs and trees can be invaluable. In terms of light and shade *deciduous* trees have the huge advantage of offering light penetration during the darkness of winter and canopies of shade during the intensity of summer.

Comfort and reassurance

The two concerns of providing comfort and reassurance are founded in both physical and psychological needs. It could be argued that they are not primarily about *aesthetic* experience, but (for example) the tactile experience of a comfortable bench and the *feeling* that one is in a safe environment imply that there *is* a connection. Moreover feelings of comfort and reassurance in a place are so fundamental to its use (or abandonment) that they must be considered as a core principle of good urban design.

Reassurance, in an urban design context, is mostly about ensuring that the layout of a space minimizes opportunities for crime and antisocial behaviour and maximizes the chances that help will be forthcoming from others in the case of victimization or an accident. Fear is a related, but separate, condition from actual risk and spaces need to be designed with fear reduction in mind. This can be achieved, for example, by minimizing the number of potential entrapment spots and designing routes so as to encourage regular passers-by along footpaths (see Shaftoe 1998 and Shaftoe and Read 2005).

Comfort is primarily achieved by providing appropriate spots in which to linger, sit, eat, drink and converse. According to analysts of effective public space (see Whyte 1980, Gehl 2003) these 'comfort' opportunities are crucial to making a place work (see page 92). Most of these activities centre around sitting spots, which may or may not be formal benches.

Figure 59 El Hospitalet neighbourhood, Barcelona

One of the non-visual aesthetic pleasures that can be enjoyed outdoors is *taste*, not so much of the landscape(!), but through eating and drinking in public spaces. Al fresco food and drink offers great sensory pleasure, perhaps harking back to our heritage as hunter-gatherers. This should be encouraged in public spaces both by providing for picnicking and liquid refreshment and through the provision of foodstalls and cafes.

Another non-visual aesthetic pleasure that can be provided for in a well-designed and managed public space is the auditory one. The delight of hearing the rustling of the wind through trees and the sound of birdsong is a welcome antidote to the urban cacophony dominated by traffic noise. However, there is also an *active* auditory dimension – that of conversation. Both Whyte (1980) and Gehl (2003) point out that opportunities for conversation need to

be appropriately *designed*. People need to be able to speak and listen without voices getting drowned out by other noises, but it also should not be so quiet that other people passing by or sitting close by can overhear the conversation.

Figure 60 Kiosk cafe, Lisbon

Natural elements

The feel of the warm breeze, or a sudden chill draft, the sound of wind through the trees, or gusts of blown autumn leaves waken the passerby to the present moment. These intense experiences of change or difference in nature – especially those that are particularly enjoyable – may provoke shared expressions of delight and pleasure. (Lennard and Lennard 1995 p39)

Figure 61 Millennium Square, Bristol

We generally feel comforted by experiencing natural elements in the landscape (Guite et al 2006). Some of this is sensed visually, but natural elements are also experienced through hearing and touch. Trees rustle and birds sing in the bushes, but perhaps the most vivid and popular sensual experience for humans is that of water (see Whyte 1980). Maybe this is to do with our evolutionary heritage from water creatures, perhaps it is the fact that our bodies consist of over 80 per cent water, or perhaps it is more symbolic. Water can offer a huge soundscape, from drips to babbling brooks to the roar of full-scale waterfalls. Furthermore, water making contact with the skin is one of the most fundamental sensory pleasures, which presumably explains the perennial popularity of splashing and paddling.

The final set of principles could be considered to be at the borderline between aesthetics and environmental psychology. These are to do with designing spaces and places that create a sense of mystery, intrigue, appropriate scale; and enclosures that are neither claustrophobic nor agoraphobic. Many of these factors interact in a synergistic manner, so although the scale and intrigue of a space may be experienced primarily visually, it will be the sound and feel of it that will reinforce that experience. Enclosure may be observed but it will also be *felt* through the microclimate it creates; likewise a place may *look* mysterious, but the sounds and smells may be subliminally affecting our perception of it.

Conclusion

Visual aesthetics dominate urban design thinking and guidance, presumably because (for those of us with good sight) what is *seen* in the environment is often the strongest sensual stimulation. But there is also a tautological factor that limits our incorporation of non-visual aspects – the term *design* comes from the same root as the French word *dessin*, meaning drawing. Urban designers' skills are therefore much more likely to be used within a visual aesthetic where they can come up with *drawn* solutions. We thus risk losing another whole palette of aesthetic experiences in the built environment – those that enhance the possibilities of delighting our senses of hearing, touch and smell. A classic example of this is the new centre promenade in Bristol, where, for reasons presumably of visual aesthetics, a faux cobbled surface has been incorporated into the vehicular highway. As a result traffic tyre noise is higher than usual, to the detriment of those trying to have conversations on the adjacent seating areas. The fountains lining the centre of the promenade, although visually intriguing, can hardly be *heard* because of the traffic noise and people are not encouraged to splash about or paddle in them. By contrast the central square of Rochefort in south-west France is almost completely pedestrianized, with consequent reduced traffic noise, and the water features are designed to positively encourage playful interaction.

Figure 62 Rochefort, France

Finally, it should be pointed out that our experience of a place is usually based on a combination of several senses. We may think, as we wander through an ancient southern European cityscape, that we are being enthralled by what we *see*, but the warm breeze against our skin and the smells of marble and roasted coffee along with the sound of conversations in exotic tongues are also contributing to our sense of place.

Maybe, if we want urban designers to pay more attention to non-visual aesthetics, we should change the name of their discipline to something that is less visually biased in its terminology!

Important Influences on the Use of Public Space

The rise and fall of the car

During the mid to late 20th century the motor car became a dominant feature in urban space.

Most North American cities and British cities such as Birmingham gave vehicles priority over pedestrians and most public spaces became polluted through-routes or parking areas. Starting in Copenhagen in 1962 (where the first conversion of a vehicular route into a pedestrian street occurred),

there has been a rolling backlash against the dominance of the motor vehicle in our towns and cities. Even Birmingham, previously one of the most car-friendly cities in Europe, is gradually reclaiming urban space for pedestrians, now that it is generally understood that the presence of internal combustion engines is not conducive to conviviality. This is nicely illustrated when streets are briefly reclaimed for other uses, as may be the case for a festival, celebration or demonstration.

Once a street has been permanently reclaimed from vehicular traffic, cafes and stalls can spill out on to it and new surface treatments can be installed.

Figure 63 Chicago

Figure 64 Streets Alive Festival, Bristol

Figure 65 Street Party, Bristol

People attracting people

As a species we are sociable animals who like to gather in groups or packs. Thus, when we see people like us lingering in a space, we are attracted to it, over and above any physical or environmental attractions that the place may have. An example of this is shown in Figure 66. Bereft of people sitting on the grass this site would look dreary and unappealing, but as people are already there (taking advantage of one of the few areas of grass in a city centre), we are attracted to it, in a self-reinforcing cycle. Significantly, the space is large enough to allow a variety of users to share it comfortably (young people in the back ground and older people from an ethnic minority in the foreground).

Thus it becomes tautological that convivial spaces tend to be full of people looking at ease. It should therefore not be surprising that nearly all the convivial spaces portrayed in this book are well populated.

Wanting to be in the presence of other people appears to be based on several psychological needs. As mentioned earlier, we are a sociable species (on the whole!) and therefore feel at home with other people around (Whyte 1988). As Lennard and Lennard (1995) observe: 'Human beings require and depend on contact with other human beings. It is self-evident that to be in the presence of other human beings is reassuring! Perceiving their presence −

Figure 66 College Green, Bristol

Figure 67 La Rambla: one of the great places for experiencing the theatre of public life (including street entertainment and real-life crime!)

through looking, hearing and touching – enables all to experience themselves as less alone' (p84). If we do need to escape the crowds, we can do this in our private dwellings or by going to the countryside. Some people, most notably extreme introverts and agoraphobics, feel uncomfortable in crowds, but this is a minority in any population. And indeed introverts generally enjoy observing others, even if they feel awkward being too visible themselves, which brings us on to the next psychological need – people-watching. For various reasons, including social learning, mate-seeking and simple voyeurism (in the positive sense), we enjoy observing other people going about their business and

leisure. This is exemplified by the popularity of reality television shows, but the best reality show is that found in well-used public spaces with provision for endlessly watching the world go by at no cost. This people-watching phenomenon is formalized in southern Europe in the slow mass promenading along certain city streets and squares in the evening (known in Italian as *la passeggiata* and in Spanish as *el paseo*) or even in the daytime, as down La Rambla in Barcelona.

Another example of this people-watching enthusiasm is the popularity of pavement cafes (see Figure 68).

Figure 68 Amsterdam

Another reason why people attract people is the need to herd together for safety. There is little more scary than a deserted city centre at night; people tend to congregate in spaces or use streets that already have other people in them as an assurance that there are 'capable guardians' (Felson and Clarke 1998). The exception would be when the city streets are dominated by groups of people behaving aggressively or threateningly, which is partly why there is such a strong argument for encouraging mixed (both demographically and activity-wise) use of public spaces (Worpole and Greenhalgh 1996). This need to feel safe in public spaces is particularly salient for young people, who are demographically most at risk of becoming victims of street crime (Shaftoe 2004).

Climate

When the enlightened planners of Copenhagen started closing off traffic-clogged streets and encouraged bars and cafes to put tables and chairs out on the streets, cynics told them that 'we are Danes, not Italians'. However, as more and more streets and squares were returned to pedestrian-only use, outdoor cafe seating and occupancy increased proportionately (see Gehl and Gemzoe 1996). It is easy to linger outside in southern Europe and the tropics (Figure 69) – although it can sometimes get *too* hot (Figure 70)!

Despite the less favourable weather conditions, alfresco sitting has become more and more popular in northern Europe. And

Figure 69 Alfama, Lisbon

Figure 70 Havana, Cuba

Figure 71 Torquay, Devon

Figure 72 Souk, Marrakech, Morocco

Source: Kathryn Smith

it is telling that when southern European language students come to the UK they still happily gather outdoors (Figure 71).

Many convivial spaces have good microclimates engendered by the enclosure effect of low-rise buildings and even when the temperature drops, people can keep warm in suitable clothing and with the support of outdoor heaters. If the worst comes to the worst, convivial spaces can be totally or partially roofed.

Cities closer to the equator also need protection from the harshness of the climate, from the searing heat rather than the bitter cold. Shade and ventilation can achieve a cooling effect, removing the need to resort to air-conditioning.

What attracts us

Significantly, nearly all our initial cues about whether we find a place convivial will be based on *visual* perception (although smell and noise could be lesser factors).

However, these initial visual cues (resulting from the design, management and usage of the space in question) trigger various psychological reactions ranging along a continuum from fear and unease (leading to a desire to escape from the space) to delight and comfort (leading to a desire to linger and enjoy the space).

Figure 73 Amsterdam

Most literature and guidance about good public spaces comes from a design perspective, although the authors of such publications usually accept that good design of the urban fabric is not an end in itself, but a means to engendering feelings of wellbeing and delight in the citizens who use squares and piazzas. Francis Tibbalds, in his seminal work *Making People-friendly Towns*, suggests that such places should consist of 'a rich, vibrant, mixed-use environment, that does not die at night or at weekends and is visually stimulating and attractive to residents and visitors alike'. John Billingham and Richard Cole, in their *Good Place Guide*, chose case studies that answered affirmatively to the following questions; 'is the

place enjoyable – is it safe, human in scale, with a variety of uses?; is it environmentally friendly – sunlit, wind- and pollution-free?; is it memorable and identifiable – distinctive?; is it appropriate – does it relate to its context?; is access freely available?' (p0.11).

Location

The other key factor that determines whether people are drawn to use certain public spaces is their location. Geographical factors can often override design and other considerations, as is the case with College Green in Bristol (see Bristol case study). This triangular public space, wedged between the cathedral, the town hall and an arterial road could not be regarded as a particularly attractive place from a design point of view and the management positively discourages certain uses, most notably skateboarding. Yet the green is hugely popular with a primarily, but not exclusively, young population, by virtue, I believe, of its location close to the centre of the city where most public transport converges.

Figure 74 College Green, Bristol

Figure 75 Earswick, York – new covered water trough as a rather pointless public space feature

If a public space is in an isolated, underpopulated or difficult-to-access location, however well-designed and managed it may be, it will not thrive. As William Whyte (1988) points out, 'The real estate people are right about location, location, location. For a space to function truly well it must be central to the constituency it is to serve – and if not in physical distance, in visual accessibility' (p128).

Ken Worpole (in Gallacher 2005) suggests that public spaces work best in urban areas that have mixed use. It is much more difficult to create convivial spaces in primarily residential areas, as was found in the 'Five Spaces for Glasgow' project (described in Gallacher 2005). The exception might be a pocket park, combined with an imaginative play space.

Attempts to create public spaces in new low-density suburbs may look good on master plans but may well become meaningless and underused in reality.

Size, Shapes and Types of Public Space

Does size matter?

In terms of overall surface area, there do seem to be some key dimensions that make a public space feel convivial. If the space is very large (such as the Plaza de la Revolución in Havana, Red Square in Moscow or even Trafalgar Square in London), the place may inspire awe, but it will not feel cosy. Most big squares, such as

these, were built by rulers as political statements of their power and influence, rather than being intended as friendly places for people to meet in. Such places do have their useful functions as places of mass assembly and demonstration. On the other hand, if a space is too small, it can feel claustrophobic and not have enough surface area to allow for convivial activities and encounters. In my view, the most convivial spaces in Central London, for example, are relatively small, but do 'breathe out' through their surrounding linking spaces.

Figure 76 St Christopher's Place, off Oxford Street, London

Several writers on urban design have suggested optimum dimensions (Lynch 1971, Alexander 1977, Gehl 2003). Kevin Lynch suggests between 12 and 24m along each side as the ideal size for a small space, going up to about 100m for large squares; Jan Gehl suggests a similar maximum and points out that the maximum distance for being able to distinguish facial expressions is about 25m. Christopher Alexander suggests that a small public square should never be more than 22m across. Steve Abley (Abley and Hill 2004) notes that the maximum distance for seeing any human movement is 135m: 'Medieval squares had average dimensions of 57 x 140 metres which indicates that we previously designed public spaces based on "social distances" but have lost these design skills over time' (p9.5).

Shape

People seem to like a bit of intrigue in their surroundings – repetition and bland facades do not stimulate the eye (Cooper Marcus and Francis 1998). Yet we also seek coherence and sense, beautifully expressed in a slogan seen in the window of a shop extolling the virtues of their custom-made fitted kitchens: 'harmony without symmetry'.

Rob Krier in his book *Urban Space* (1979) spends a considerable amount of time detailing many options and variations in the shape of public space. By studying numerous existing public spaces, he attempts to categorize the various types of shape that have come into existence.

Although many public spaces in British towns are called 'squares' they very rarely are, often as an incremental result of their medieval origins. Even fine symmetrical squares in Continental Europe (such as Place des Vosges in Paris and Plaza Mayor in Madrid) often feel less sterile as a result of tree planting and intriguing links to the surrounding neighbourhood.

Figure 77 Madrid: corner leading out of Plaza Mayor

Curves and bends in public spaces offer intrigue and the prospect of something interesting round the corner. This was the basis for Gordon Cullen's (1961) thinking about successful townscapes that revealed themselves sequentially rather than being all there at once. And as Hundertwasser (see Kliczkowski 2003), the delightfully eccentric remodeller of some of Vienna's dour buildings, claimed, 'straight lines are utterly alien to human beings, to life and the whole of creation'. Christopher Alexander (2004a), in his work on morphogenesis, also notes that natural forms are hardly ever rectangular, let alone square. It must also be of significance that many of the most popular pieces of architecture (such as Gaudi's in Barcelona, the Sydney Opera House, the Guggenheim Museum in Bilbao and the 'Gherkin' in London) are curvaceous.

Types of public space

A broad definition of public space would cover anywhere that is universally accessible to citizens and could therefore include everything from national parks to town hall foyers. Mean and Tims (2005) take a radical approach to identifying public space and include such things as car-boot sales and arts centres under this banner. However, as mentioned earlier, this book focuses on the middle range of urban spaces that are used as general gathering and breathing places. Although there is some overlap, in the following paragraphs I identify the types of space that can perform these functions in a convivial way.

Figure 78 Smaller square leading off the main market square, Krakow, Poland

Open squares

These are the classical places where people have gathered throughout history and they still epitomize most people's stereotype of public space. Even within this typology, there is a huge range of sizes, shapes and functions (see Krier 1979).

Enclosed and/or covered spaces

Primarily for reasons of the vagaries of the climate, some successful public spaces are partially or totally covered. Some of these are truly public (as with the Winter Gardens in Sheffield); others have another primary function – often as a transport interchange or marketplace, but are still accessible to and usable by any members of the public. The huge covered foyer area of Madrid's revamped Atocha Station is a fine example of this.

Rather more contentious are the huge 'private' public spaces that have burgeoned in many North American and European cities over the last few decades. Although these malls have some characteristics of urban public space, they are usually privately owned

Figure 79 Plaça Reial, Barcelona – a classic open square, but with arcading for shade and protection

Figure 80 Atocha Station concourse, Madrid

Figure 81 Privately owned space: The Bullring, Birmingham

and are primarily targeted for use by consumers. The owners don't want people to just hang around there – they want them to spend money and everything is designed explicitly or subtly to facilitate this. They are therefore much more controlled than a true public space, with restrictions on activities that are not purely consumptive – busking and demonstrating, for example. They are also likely to be heavily monitored by day and sealed off at night. They offer then a kind of sanitized version of public space, without any of the rough edges or unpredictability that make true public space so vital and democratic.

Pocket parks and green spaces

Quite apart from the aesthetic and amenity aspect of small areas of soft landscaping in towns, greenery helps to cut down noise and pollution and also has benefits for health and wellbeing (Kellert and Wilson 1993, Guite et al 2006). The classic urban green space in the UK is the Georgian communal or public garden, surrounded by terraced houses (see Figure 82). Such spaces need a higher level of maintenance than hard landscaped areas but can prove to be very popular oases in densely built-up areas, particularly those with a high concentration of apartments.

Boulevards and linear parks

Public space may run parallel to traffic arteries or be a pedestrian route in its own right (see Jacobs 1993). The important factors are that it should give priority to pedestrian use and lingering and that there should be sufficient softening and separation from vehicular movement (usually by providing broad footpaths set back from the road with trees and other forms of landscaping). Sometimes these are built into the townscape, as with the Parisian boulevards; at others they are reclaimed from former uses, such as the green ring round the centre of Krakow which is the

Figure 82 Victoria Square, Clifton, Bristol

Figure 83 Waterford, Ireland: reclaimed public space by the river, but rather isolated by the adjacent busy traffic artery

route of the former city walls. Many maritime and riverine cities have created or reinstated waterfront promenades. Waterford in Ireland, Bideford in Devon (see CABE Space 2007) and the South Bank of the Thames in London are all examples of the rediscovery of the delights of lingering by the waterside.

One of the most inspiring and successful examples of a reclaimed linear park is the 'Promenade Plantée' in Paris, which runs along the route of an abandoned urban railway line, some of it a viaduct with new shops and workshops underneath.

Figure 84 Promenade Plantée, Paris

Figure 85 Monção, Northern Portugal

Reclaimed streets

As the motor vehicle is gradually being pushed back from the centre of cities, streets can once more become fully public spaces where people feel comfortable to linger, eat and drink, rather than scuttle along, diving into the occasional shop or cafe. Denmark was the trailblazer in this (see Gehl and Gemzoe 1996), closely followed by the French and then the rest of Europe. Now even the remotest European towns have their traffic-free streets reclaimed for the pedestrian.

Linked spaces

Some of the most enjoyable public spaces are those that consist of a series of squares connected by short pedestrian routes, so that one can wander through a series of unfurling tableaux. Sarlat Le Canéda in southern France, Algajola in Corsica, Padua in northern Italy and York (the last two are featured as case studies in this book) contain fine examples of such linked urban spaces.

CHAPTER FOUR

How Can One Create and Sustain Successful Public Spaces?

Designed or Evolved?

Given that many convivial spaces seem to have grown organically through an accumulation of adaptations and additions, can we design such places at the drawing board? Critics of formal architecture and planning such as Bernard Rudofsky (*Architecture without Architects*) and Christopher Alexander (*The Timeless Way of Building, A Pattern Language*) suggest that we are better off 'growing' good places and spaces, rather than trying to build them from a blueprint. I think we have a lot to learn about how plants and natural environments grow, evolve and adapt to local circumstances and then to mirror this in the development of the built environment. Christopher Alexander has done some fascinating research in this direction (described in *The Nature of Order*) and uses the term 'morphogenesis' to describe this more natural approach to building and development. There are some ancient and modern examples to suggest that it is possible to design convivial places as a

whole, but they tend to be relatively small in scale (see for example the Barcelona case study on page 81). The post-1947 culture of master-planning whole urban areas is less likely to accommodate the fine grain, local nuance and adaptability which seem to be at the root of convivial places.

Gradual organic growth of townscapes is often best. Some architects and planners like a blank slate. They usually do their best work, however, when they don't have one. (Abley and Hill 2006 p8.7)

The city is discussed in barren eviscerated terms and in technical jargon by urban professionals as if it were a lifeless, detached being. In fact it is a sensory, emotional, lived experience. (Landry 2006 p2)

Many of the theories and principles of urban design assume that it is a mechanistic, fixed discipline that can lead to a definitive 'master plan', arrived at through a systematic series of assessments based on land use, circulation, topography and so on.

As a result, a rigid design is produced that is implemented and then left, as the planners and designers move on to their next project. However, as the quotes above indicate, there is an alternative approach that is much more messy and incremental and thus not to the taste of the urbanist professionals who generally seem to prefer purity and finality. Sennett (1973) highlighted this unhelpful professional obsession with order when he described master plans as an attempt to produce perfect 'machines' which would (inevitably) break down because they were so rigid and could not accommodate the evolving history of human and social development: '… they have failed, not for lack of technical expertise, but because they have not had the power to be adaptive over the course of time' (p100). 'In the shaping of cities, the technological metaphor is not practical; it simply doesn't work' (p101).

In their abstruse treatise on 'space syntax' (mapping how urban spaces are used by people) Hillier and Hanson (1984 p140) do make the clear assertion that:

… it is extraordinary that unplanned growth should produce a better global order than planned redevelopment, but it seems undeniable. The inference seems unavoidable that traditional systems work because they produce a global order that responds to the requirements of a dual (inhabitants and strangers) interface, while modern systems do not work because they fail to produce it.

Rudofsky (1964) was one of the first theorists to challenge the view that a good built environment required specialists to design it in a complete way. He referred to 'the exasperatingly complicated organism that is a town', suggesting, mostly by illustrative material, that good architecture is not necessarily produced by design specialists but by the spontaneous and continuous activity of a whole people. This concept of urban design as a continuous and adaptive process, rather than a fixed science, was developed by Brand (1994) in his account of *How Buildings Learn*. In this book he is particularly critical of design as a rigid production of buildings and fixed spaces and gives, as an alternative approach, examples of what he terms 'low road' environments which are much more amenable to adaptation to the messiness of life and inevitable social evolution.

Lennard and Lennard (1995) liken a well-designed city to a healthy organism where individual cells modify and adapt themselves in response to continuous feedback loops with other parts of the organism: ' … a healthy city is one in which finely tuned mechanisms exist for recognising the needs of every individual, and group, and for responding appropriately to those needs' (p22). Clearly, if you believe this, a rigid master-planning approach to urban design is not going cope with the need for constant adaptation and adjustment, with the result that the built environment will rapidly become unhealthy for most of its inhabitants.

The principal proselytizer of good urban design as an organic growth process is Christopher Alexander, commencing with his book *New Theory of Urban Design* (1987) and subsequently developed in his series *The Nature of Order* (2004a). Alexander asks why our modern cities so often lack a sense of natural growth, and goes on to suggest a set of rules and guidelines by which we can inject that organic character back into our high streets, buildings and squares.

In the light of this discussion, it is telling that one of the most successful urban design initiatives in Europe – the reclaiming of the historic heart of Copenhagen through pedestrianization of streets and the creation of a series of linked squares, was achieved incrementally, with no overall master plan (Gehl and Gemzoe 1996).

Figure 86 Copenhagen city centre

The contrast between a master-planned, fixed urban design approach and a more incremental organic one is not just a question of two different styles of treatment; it is more fundamental than that. It is the difference between a top-down, controlling system of dealing with the built environment and a bottom-up, democratic one. Furthermore it will affect whether people have to adapt to a predetermined environment or whether the environment can be adapted to best meet people's needs. Sennett (1973) points out that the origins of master-planning can be traced back to Hausmann's redesign of Paris, which was explicitly aimed at giving the ruling class a better means of controlling the seething masses, by creating broad and straight routes that would facilitate the speedy deployment of armed forces. As Sennett also relates in *Flesh and Stone* (1994), Nash's designs for Regent Street and Regent's Park were also intended to allow the upper classes to speedily pass by the lower orders hanging around on street corners. One of Sennett's theses is that this separation and control of 'other' populations is actually dangerous in the longer term as it generates prejudice and can lead to 'big' violence (such as revolutions and riots) rather than the small everyday conflicts that are actually a healthy way of people getting to know, understand and accommodate each other. He therefore argues that a certain amount of disorder is actually a good thing and that the planners' desire to order and predestine human function is doomed to failure or worse – violence.

The very term master-planning is telling in itself, implying as it does a masculine, dominating system, where an elite who have allegedly 'mastered' the science of creating an effective built environment impose their worldview on the ordinary citizenry. Landry (2006) asserts that city-making is not a science, it is an art, preferably created by '… the people who populate the city. They mould the physical into shape and frame its use and how it feels' (p5).

It is no coincidence that much of the literature on this alternative approach to urban design regards a good built environment as an *organism* rather than a *machine*. Historically, with the exception of a few planned defensive or military settlements (such as Richelieu's in France), most towns and cities just grew organically. Undoubtedly this led to problems such as congestion and strained infrastructure, but the reaction in the 19th and 20th centuries was arguably too extreme.

On the one hand was the planned city movement led by visionaries such as Ebenezer Howard, complemented later by the modernist urbanist movement spearheaded by Le Corbusier. These people had the best intentions to provide people with hygienic, purified environments for work, rest and play but in their more extreme forms their plans led to sterile, alienating, mechanistic environments from which we still reap negative social consequences (see for example Hartcliffe in Bristol or Bijlmermeer in Amsterdam).

Even when these environments have not become places of misery and last resort, they are still soulless locations with very little human stimulation (consider the Coventry City Centre Precinct before its recent costly redevelopment, Les Halles and La Défense in Paris or central Milton Keynes). These examples were master-planned to within an inch of their life; allowing for very little easy adjustment once their dysfunctions became apparent.

There are a few examples of new master-planned urban spaces that do seem to work as vibrant locations to hang out in (see for example the new Potsdamer Platz described in the Berlin case study). One American design practice, the Jerde Partnership International, has made its reputation by 'creating places to *be*'. Tellingly John Jerde asserts that 'what we seek to create are inviting, evocative places where people feel safe, comfortable and happy; unique places

Figure 87 Horton Plaza, San Diego, designed by Jerde Partnership International

that speak to a site's climate, context and culture; genial places where variegated populations gather to have a fantastic time' (Jerde 1998 p69). It is not casually that he uses the adjective 'fantastic', as the defining feature of Jerde's urban spaces is a high level of fantasy; in fact critics of his approach describe his work as 'Disney-like' and one of his most famous places is CityWalk at the Universal Studios in Los Angeles – a kind of recreated urban street encrusted with colour and variety. It is this use of colour and an almost overwhelming variety of styles and spatial treatments that gives his new spaces a feeling of incremental accretion, rather than the master-planned uniformity that makes so many new urban spaces look sterile.

The 'organic' urban designs, as espoused by Alexander and others, can 'bend with the wind', be 'pruned and grafted', will 'adapt to the prevailing conditions' and many other plant-like analogies. In his Schumacher lecture of 2004 (partial transcript available from www.livingneighbourhoods.org), Alexander argued that what he calls the morphogenetic approach to urban design is the only true form of built-environment sustainability, because it produces a *wholeness* for the future that is the physical manifestation of our social and cultural aspirations. The concept of morphogenesis is a biological one, to explain that any living organism is an evolving system in which what is changing in the organism is always drawn from the form of what *was* in the moment just before. He points out that traditional societies always took a morphogenetic approach to the

development of the built environment: 'Whatever it was, it was shaped, modified, shaped again, and adjusted and so on and so forth. As a result of the morphogenesis and the complex adaptation that was possible under these conditions, the places people made had *life*' (Alexander 2004b p6). He then goes on to give an example of the morphogenetic evolution of St Mark's Square in Venice, one of the most beautiful public spaces in the world.

So if this organic, incremental approach to urban design appears to lead to so much more 'people-friendly' environments, why do we do so little of it? Part of the answer lies in the way we have set up the suite of built-environment professions and the legislation that supports (or inhibits) them. As Brand (1994) points out, very few architects and planners revisit the developments they helped to form to see how they have fared over the years. The cynic would argue that they don't want to have their noses rubbed in the mess they have created, but there is a more sober interpretation, which is that there is just no incentive for them to go back and see how their buildings and spaces have 'learnt'. Even if they could be persuaded to go back there is the likelihood that in their arrogance they will blame the users for not treating their creations correctly (according to the instructions and ideology) or, if they are humble enough to admit their mistakes, there will be no money left to modify things, as the snagging period will have long since expired. On top of this is all the suffocating legislation, from planning through to building codes and regulations, which create a very rigid system of predetermined strategies and designs. As Alexander (2004b p6) comments:

The idea that we have inherited from the thinking of the last years is that when you build something, you make a plan which is so detailed that it can become a specification for a contractor and protect you in a court of law if something goes wrong with a particular line of bolts. This legal reasoning began to dominate architecture and construction – and as a result of accepting it, we slipped into a fiction which was that it is actually possible to make a blueprint of a piece of the environment, or the completed environment, and have it work. Now this is a fiction.

People who use the built environments created by the professionals are usually desperate to modify and personalize their surroundings. The most obvious manifestation of this is the imprinting of 'desire lines' along circulation routes not predetermined by the urban designers – the trampled flower bed on the shortest route to the main entrance of a public building or the muddy corner short cut on the way out of a landscaped car park (see Brand 1994 p187). Boudon (1969), a social researcher, visited a Le Courbusier-designed housing estate 40 years after it had been completed, to find a whole range of adaptations to the buildings and spaces, nearly all of which would be regarded as 'impurities' by the original designer.

Given that human beings are eager to adapt and personalize their environments incrementally and that the results have so much more character, usability and 'soul', surely we should be encouraging this more 'organic' approach to urban design. Such places are likely to be better used and cared for (just think of St Mark's Square in Venice, which evolved over hundreds of years), yet we are still producing too many sterile places resulting from top-down, blueprint thinking. Most European countries have abandoned the wholesale clearance and rebuild approach that characterized the immediate post-war period, but we are still not very good at developing healthy and tasteful places. Through education, modified legislation and more post-occupancy evaluation, aligned with a different resourcing system, it should be possible to operate a more organic regime to produce urban designs capable of adaptation, rather than rigid schemes that cost dearly when they are found to be defective.

Case Study: Ciutat Vella, Barcelona

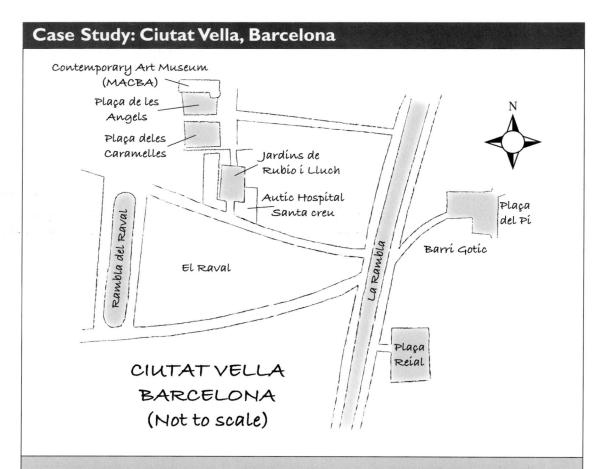

Contemporary Art Museum (MACBA)
Plaça de les Angels
Plaça deles Caramelles
Jardins de Rubio i Lluch
Autic Hospital Santa creu
Rambla del Raval
El Raval
La Rambla
Barri Gotic
Plaça del Pi
Plaça Reial

CIUTAT VELLA
BARCELONA
(Not to scale)

In the last 25 years, Barcelona has moved from a place deliberately held back by the Franco dictatorship to become one of the most progressive cities in Europe. Of particular interest, from an urban space point of view, are the improvements to the ancient central area, the Ciutat Vella, and especially El Raval, the area immediately to the west of La Rambla. The Ciutat Vella is a densely populated part of the city, consisting mostly of old apartment buildings rising up to five storeys above stores and workshops, built along very narrow streets. To the east of the famous Rambla (an iconic public space in its own right) lies the Barri Gotic, an ancient neighbourhood punctuated with a number of convivial spaces, such as Plaça del Pi.

Further down La Rambla, Plaça Reial is a formal, arcaded square that despite its pleasant appearance had a reputation for crime and antisocial activities. As a result of some refurbishment and a constant police presence, it is now a much safer place, lined with cafes and public seating.

Figure 88 Plaça del Pi. This square is regularly filled with market stalls, cafe tables and buskers

The whole of El Raval, on the other side of La Rambla, was considered a no-go area for many years. Despite its historic status, the neighbourhood was dominated by drug dealers and users, prostitutes and petty criminals. Since the 1980s the municipality has intervened drastically to 'normalize' the area, with some considerable success – at least in the northern half of the neighbourhood. The intervention has mostly consisted of selective demolition and rebuilding of some parts to create new urban spaces, workplaces (such as new university buildings, publishing offices and galleries) and new homes for residents of the cleared buildings who wanted to stay in the area. The most striking change is the creation of several new public squares (usually with car parking underneath), formed by the removal of entire blocks of problematic tenements.

Figure 89 Plaça Reial: police presence, but a pity they feel they have to sit in their cars!

Figure 90 Plaça Reial: New street furniture has offered both formal and informal sitting opportunities

Thanks to its close working relationship with community organizations and its commitment to accommodating the existing resident population, the programme of improvement in El Raval seems to be succeeding in upgrading the area without the wholesale gentrification process that occurs in many other high-value inner urban areas in Europe.

Figure 91 Rambla del Raval: a new square created by the demolition of a complete city block of old buildings

Figure 92 Plaça dels Angels. This square, created next to the new Contemporary Art Museum in the heart of El Raval, has proved to be a popular gathering place for young people

Figure 93 Plaça de les Caramelles: a new square primarily for the residents of the new social housing blocks that surround it

Comfort

Seating

Probably the single most important provision to ensure a successful public space is a sufficient range of opportunities for sitting. William Whyte's (1988) groundbreaking research into successful public spaces tested various possibilities, such as location and size, to establish what were the key factors that differentiated successful (i.e. well-used) public spaces from unsuccessful ones. He concluded: 'No matter how many other variables we checked, one basic point kept coming through. We at last recognized that it was the major one: *People tend to sit most where there are places to sit*' (p110).

Figure 95 Sheffield

But despite the willingness of people to apparently sit almost anywhere (Figure 94), the built environment is littered with seating of the wrong type, in the wrong place, with the result that it is rarely used (Figure 95): The main problem seems to be that public space designers and providers not only provide the wrong type of sitting opportunities, but, crucially, they put fixed seating in the wrong places (Figures 96, 97).

Figure 94 Central Bristol

Figure 96 Birmingham

Figure 97 Budapest

Generally people sitting down like to observe rather than be observed (particularly from behind), so seats without a wall or other barrier behind them are likely to be underused (Figure 98).

As with shoes, for seating there is no 'one size fits all'. Different people require different seating types and locations according to circumstances. Therefore it is important to provide a range of seating opportunities in any public space and for seating to be flexible and adaptable.

In many cases, the best seating does not actually consist of custom-designed benches or chairs, rather horizontal surfaces that serve multiple functions. Broad steps are a classic example of this (Figures 99, 100).

Orientation is a crucial factor as to whether steps (and other horizontal sitting surfaces) will become popular. In northern climates they should be south-facing to catch the sun; in southern climates the converse is true. They should also offer some kind of spectacle – usually a street scene – as steps in particular make an ideal grandstand.

Conventional seating arrangements, with suitable protection behind, may appeal to older people (Figure 101).

Figure 98 Temple Quarter, Bristol

Figure 99 Budapest

Figure 100 Bristol

Figure 101 Barcelona

Vantage points

As mentioned earlier, one of the things that people enjoy about public space is to be able to 'watch the world go by' or more specifically to observe other people. For this reason, good vantage points are cherished, even if it means subverting the conventional arrangements for seating and use.

This seems to be a universal phenomenon, as Figures 102–108 demonstrate. It is therefore important that seats and their surroundings should be designed to allow this, rather than assume that people will only sit in the obvious place.

Figure 102 Barcelona

Figure 103 Bristol

Figure 104 Vietnam

Source:
Vietnam photo: Kathy Sykes

Figure 105 Krakow

Figure 106 Padua

Figure 107 Padua

Figure 108 Bristol

Shelter and protection

The vagaries of the climate mean that in many areas seating will need to be at least partially protected from cold winds or bright sunshine. As Figures 109–112 show, there are various innovative approaches, from partial screening right up to total enclosure and creation of a winter garden.

Figure 109 Glass-fronted seating area, Bristol

Figure 110 Canopy over seating, Budapest

Figure 111 Traditional shelter, Minehead, Somerset

Figure 112 Winter Garden, Sheffield

Movable seating

One of the most exciting possibilities with seating is to provide chairs that users can move about and group as they wish (Whyte 1988). At a stroke this overcomes the difficulty that urban designers have of locating seating appropriately. Different people will want to sit in different ways according to who they are with and the weather conditions, for example. Generally it is thought that movable seating can only be provided in areas that can be secured at night (for example the Jardin du Luxembourg, Paris, and Parade Gardens, Bath, Figures 113 and 114).

However there are examples where movable seating has been provided in completely permeable public areas, such as the River Danube waterfront walk in Budapest, where cast-iron seats, which can be dragged into new positions but would be difficult to run away with, have been provided (Figure 115).

Lennard and Lennard (1995 p46) describe how the city of Munich took the 'bold and imaginative step' of providing movable chairs in a couple of its central squares: 'Critics who warned that the chairs would be stolen or vandalised have, happily, been proved wrong. The chairs are enormously popular and have contributed significantly to the success of Munich's pedestrian zone.'

Figure 113 Jardin du Luxembourg, Paris

Figure 114 Parade Gardens, Bath

Figure 115 Budapest, Hungary

Figure 116 Venice

Leaning

Sometimes people don't want to go as far as to sit down, either because they want to survey the scene from a standing position or because they are only intending to pause briefly. Leaning places are therefore a small but valued part of the public realm (see Whyte 1980). These leaning opportunities usually are a by-product of their core function, which may be a piece of public art, plinth, bollard or suitable wall.

Figure 117 Padua

Comfort breaks

It is hardly the most glamorous of subjects for urban designers and policy makers to deal with, but adequate provision of suitable public toilets is part of the fundamental infrastructure for successful public spaces (see Greed 2003). Many local authorities seem to regard public toilets as a liability (and drain on their resources), rather than an asset and there has been a worrying trend of closure over the last few decades. Inadequate toilet provision has a particularly discriminatory effect against older people, those with children and people with disabilities (Holland et al 2007).

Eating and drinking

Food and drink outlets can attract people to a public space. These can range from cafes and bars with outside tables to portable refreshment kiosks where people can get takeaways to be consumed in adjacent sitting areas.

Figure 118 Park Güell, Barcelona

There could also be suitable places for picnics, even if not specifically designated as such. Such spaces either need grass or suitable perching places, some shelter (from sun or wind) and a reasonable aspect. Sometimes the mere addition of a food outlet and a few tables can transform somewhere into a convivial space, as the photograph of a vacant building lot in Berlin demonstrates (Figure 120).

One important factor to be considered is the provision of suitable litter bins and their regular emptying. Public spaces can rapidly appear unappealing if they are strewn with discarded food and drink containers or overflowing bins.

A disturbing trend in the UK has been the imposition of by-laws to prohibit the consumption of alcohol in designated public spaces. This is a blunt instrument aimed at banning street drinking alcoholics from the public realm, but it potentially affects all of us. And as Ken Worpole (2007) points out, street-drinkers are citizens too and, as long as they are causing no harm to others, they should have a legitimate right to frequent public space. He goes on to suggest that by deregulating some public spaces or parts of them, this 'looseness' or 'slackness' could perform a necessary and useful social function. This could also apply to groups of young people who just want to hang out or skateboard.

Figure 119 Picnickers, Lisbon, Portugal

Figure 120 Impromptu food court, East Berlin

Case Study: Berlin

Since German reunification in 1990, Berlin has been the subject of a huge amount of reconstruction, particularly in the former east zone where the following two examples of remodelled public space are situated.

Potsdamer Platz

The Potsdamer Platz, not far from the Brandenburg Gate (and therefore at the heart of reunified Berlin), has been completely remodelled as a primarily commercial area (offices, retail and leisure) but with a significant public space component.

The most intriguing of these quasi-public spaces is the Sony Centre, which has been constructed from scratch as a huge, semi-enclosed town square (see Flierl 2002, Leier 2004). Although this centre is an open access space, with places where people can just hang out, Flierl (2002 p24) is critical of its primarily consumption-based and controlled function, describing it as being conceived along the lines of Disneyland, as a theme park – 'its theme was city and downtown, but it is not a real city and downtown, only a virtual one.'

Figure 121 A winning combination of public art, water and eating opportunities

Figure 122 Huge all-age see-saws

Figure 123 Sony Centre

Marzahn

A very different location is Marzahn, a former East German housing estate at the easternmost fringe of the Berlin conurbation. A concerted attempt was made by the Berlin municipality to bring colour, variety and vitality to this dreary peripheral neighbourhood, in order to prevent its slide into undesirability and decline. As well as work on remodelling the housing, considerable effort was put into creating lively and intriguing public spaces.

The whole regeneration project was subtitled '*der Stadtteil mit Farbe*' (the neighbourhood with colour), to emphasize the principle of bringing colour and delight into people's lives by adding actual colour to the built fabric – such a simple but effective approach.

Figure 124 Seating and public art rolled into one

Figure 125 Mosaic mural and flower planting

Figure 126 Sandpit and colourful housing as a backdrop

Figure 127 Play space enlivened by murals

Joy

One of the characteristics that differentiates successful from avoided public spaces (and indeed is at the heart of the notion of conviviality) is the range of opportunities they provide for the experience of joy or delight. Some of this pleasure is achieved by watching or interacting with other people, but this can be enhanced by providing focal points to draw people in and encourage them to linger. This can be achieved broadly in three ways – through the provision of good hard and soft landscaping, public art and entertainment. As well as being ends in themselves, they often provide the catalyst for an impromptu conversation between strangers.

Hard and soft landscaping

The selection of the right kind of surfacing and cladding materials can have a substantial effect on the success of a public space. Vast areas of concrete and tarmac do not offer much delight, yet these are the principle surfacing materials in too many public spaces. Materials need to look good, yet be durable, as a successful public space will get a lot of usage. High quality materials such as marble and granite, although expensive, may prove to be economical in the long term, as they are more resistant to wear and weathering.

Soft landscaping (in the form of plants, shrubs and trees), can be a great source of delight, as well as offering health and

Figure 128 Zurich, Switzerland

practical benefits (see for example Kaplan and Kaplan 1989, Hough 1989). Well-considered planting can: soften the hardness of surrounding buildings, frame views and vistas, provide boundary treatments, moderate pollution, have a calming effect on users, introduce variety and seasonal difference and offer a more comfortable microclimate. This latter point is a particular bonus of deciduous trees; in the summer they offer shade from bright sunlight and in the winter they shed their leaves to maximize the availability of natural light.

Colour

It should also be remembered that colour brings joy, particularly in northern climates where grey skies and low light predominate for much of the year (Mahnke 1987).

Figure 129 Neal's Yard, Covent Garden, London

When asked, people prefer colourful environments (see Duttmann et al 1981). Yet most architecture and urban design is drearily monochromatic. It seems as though designers have enough to think about without the added complication of colour, when for a remarkably small capital outlay, buildings and spaces can be transformed through the imaginative use of colour (see Marzahn, Berlin case study).

When Albania, the poorest country in Europe, became liberated from Soviet control, the mayor of the capital city wanted to brighten up people's lives, so he did it literally – by the cheap but highly visible transformation of the existing built environment through colourful painting of exterior surfaces.

When people are left to their own devices in the built environment, one of the first things they will do is brighten up their surroundings with paint and murals. One of

Figure 130 Burano, Veneto region

the most famous examples of this is Burano in the Venetian lagoon, where local fishermen have competed with each other to paint their houses brightly.

In Vienna, renegade artist Friedensreich Hundertwasser was encouraged by an enlightened mayor to remodel buildings and structures using colour and soft landscaping, with spectacular results (see Figure 132 overleaf; also Kliczkowski 2003).

Figure 131
Tirana, Albania

Source:
Tobias Woldendorp

Figure 132 Hundertwasser House, Vienna

Source: Angela Hull

Public art

Public art is a well-established presence in public space. Historically, this has been of the monumental kind, usually to commemorate some great event or famous person. This triumphalist approach has, in the last few decades, been increasingly replaced by a more populist and often witty type of art (see Lennard and Lennard 1995). Usually this will consist of a sturdy sculpture or mural.

Figure 133 Grafton Street, Dublin

Figure 134 Millennium Square, Bristol

Figure 135 Rue du Midi, Brussels

In Brussels the city administration has a proactive policy of commissioning murals to brighten up drab gable end walls throughout the city centre (Figure 135).

Rather more contentious is the notion of informal public art, which usually takes the form of graffiti or stencilling. There are mixed views about whether such works constitute vandalism or art and this will vary according to the quality of the result. However, there is a danger that authorities take a blanket stand against any form of guerrilla art, when some of it actually enhances the public realm, as can be seen in Figures 136–138.

Figure 136 This mural by the artist Banksy appeared without permission in central Bristol and has subsequently become a visitor attraction

Figure 137 This graffiti in a Paris street has brightened up a drab concrete end wall

Figure 138 This huge mural in Zaragoza was painted on a partially demolished structure that was to be redeveloped

Public art fixtures (such as murals and sculptures) need to be robust and resilient and should not offer invitations to defacement. The rather brutal sculpture in a Lisbon street (Figure 139) has been made even less attractive by graffiti and fly-posting.

Public art should have an immediate appeal and not be so esoteric that citizens do not know what it is.

The rather miserable-looking 'seating sculpture' in Edinburgh reminded me of the importance of context when furnishing the built environment. Concrete is not much fun to lie on in Scotland – it is too cold and damp, whereas an almost identical structure I came across in Barcelona was hugely popular – presumably the weather made it more comfortable to lounge on.

Figure 139 Lisbon, Portugal

Figure 140 Is it a seat? Is it a sculpture? Holyrood, Edinburgh

Figure 141 Sculptural 'recliner': Barcelona waterfront, with Frank Gehry's big fish sculpture in the background

Entertainment

As with public art, there has been a long history of street entertainment. This can consist of formal events such as festivals and bandstand concerts, or through the enabling of busking and informal events such as bric-a-brac stalls and demonstrations. Such events often make city administrators nervous as they are not predictable and can be messy. However, they are a low-cost way to bring public spaces to life with the minimum of regulation, they can offer substantial social and democratic benefits.

Figure 142 La Rambla, Barcelona

Figure 143 Street band, Krakow, Poland

A number of municipal administrations have set up licensing (e.g. Covent Garden, London, and Bath) or simple regulatory contracts (e.g. Berne in Switzerland) to ensure the quality and benignity of street entertainment. However, except in areas of high demand, street entertainment is usually self-regulatory, insofar as people will soon lose interest in poor quality acts and any behaviour which causes substantial offence can always be dealt with by existing laws.

It is therefore surprising that more street entertainment is not encouraged, whether proactively by organizing events or simply by designating spaces for buskers and so on, as it is an almost no-cost way to bring colour, joy and delight to public spaces and there seems to be an endless potential supply of artists and performers eager to exercise their talents in public. Perhaps this is a case of nobody in most municipalities actually having the responsibility or inclination to encourage this kind of animation.

Figure 144 Folk dancing, Budapest

Case Study: Bristol

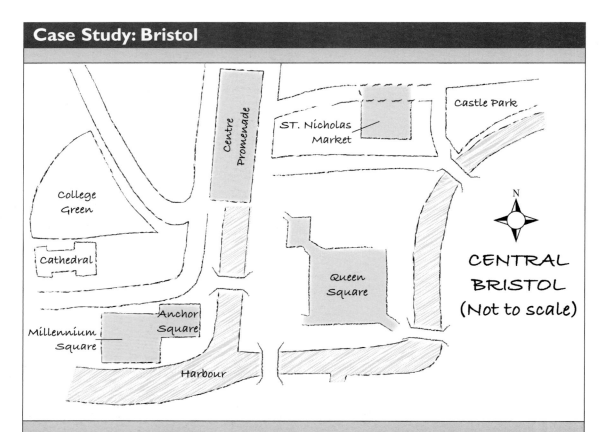

Bristol, in south-west England, has a population of 400,000. The central area is particularly well endowed with public spaces, both old and new.

Figure 145 Queen Square

Queen Square was completed in Georgian times and is a large formal square. Although visually impressive, it is underused for much of the time. Additional seating has been put in, but it only really comes alive when special events are mounted there. Part of the problem is that it is probably too large to be a convivial space; the other problem is that nearly all the terraced buildings surrounding the square are used as offices,

Figure 146 St Nicholas Markets

Figure 147 College Green

Figure 148 Centre Promenade

so there is very little life to spill out on to the open space except at lunchtimes.

The St Nicholas Markets area is a partially covered Victorian space, which benefits from a wide variety of activities, including cafes and stalls, with the result that during daylight hours it is always buzzing with activity.

College Green is sandwiched between the Council House (Town Hall), the cathedral and one of Bristol's main shopping streets. Despite its relatively bland design, its central location and degree of greenery makes it one of Bristol's most successful gathering places, particularly for young people, but also for all ages. The Green was vastly improved by the removal of a through road that passed between the Council House and the cathedral (along the left-hand side of Figure 147).

Until 2000, the Centre Promenade was essentially the centre of a huge traffic circulation system. The space was extensively remodelled with new seating, planting and a water feature (the latter

Figure 149 Millennium Square

Figure 150 Millennium Square

being rather ironic insofar as the space is a huge concrete slab spanning part of the ancient harbour). Attempts were made to downgrade and slow the traffic but this has not been entirely successful, with the result that this is still a noisy and somewhat exposed place to be.

Millennium Square and its linked neighbour, Anchor Square, are recent additions to Bristol's cityscape. The Square straddles a large underground car-park and this has limited the amount of feasible soft landscaping. The result is a big shiny space that has a rather clinical feel to it. Its saving grace is a number of water features which are popular cooling-off and paddling places when the weather is warm.

Managing and Maintaining Public Spaces

Arguably, the way public spaces are managed (and animated) is as crucial to their success as their physical attributes. As suggested in the section on inclusion versus exclusion (page 16), places can be managed with a heavy or light touch. Some commentators (see for example Wood 1981, Holland et al 2007) note that if places are over-regulated in an oppressive manner they become less convivial and, indeed, quite intimidating, even for people who are there perfectly legally. The widespread use of CCTV in the UK has come under some criticism, not only from civil liberties groups, but also from those who have questioned its value as a crime prevention tool (see Shaftoe 2002, Welsh and Farrington 2002).

Figure 151 CCTV monitoring centre, southern England

Similarly, heavy formal policing of public spaces can make them feel uncomfortable for certain users.

Figure 152 South-west England

Of course, in places notorious for illegal or intimidating activity, it may be necessary, at least for a while, to resort to formal social control, as for example in Barcelona's Plaça Reial – see case study on page 88.

Figure 153 Park keepers, Padua

Figure 154 Park keepers, Bologna

In response to the perceived need to have 'more eyes on the streets' the Dutch Government supported municipalities in the training and appointment of 'city guards' (*stadswachten*). These were people, often from the long-term unemployed register, who were trained, put in uniforms and then given the task of advising and reassuring members of the public, while patrolling streets, public spaces and public transport. This approach spread to other European states and arrived in the UK under the guise of 'street wardens', eventually taking the role of 'Police Community Support Officers' in many British towns.

As mentioned earlier (see page 21), a number of British cities have taken other innovative approaches to managing and policing their public spaces by employing street wardens or 'ambassadors' – uniformed staff who can provide advice and reassurance to users of public spaces, while also dealing with day-to-day management issues.

In some Italian cities, even more innovative approaches have been taken in terms of staffing public space. The city of Padua employs retired people on a part-time basis to keep an eye on their urban parks, while in Bologna volunteers are recruited from immigrant groups to act as park keepers. This latter approach achieves a double benefit of both providing a reassuring official presence in public spaces and altering indigenous citizens' stereotypical view of immigrants as being potentially problematic.

Worpole and Knox (2007) note that citizens have a remarkable capacity for self-regulation. As long as a public space is not totally out of control or completely dominated by one faction, members of the public normally find ways of accommodating their different needs and informally enforcing acceptable behaviour.

Another successful UK management initiative in recent years has been the appointment of town-centre managers. Although they often have a remit to improve the economic prospects of town centres, obviously this can include improving the quality and attractiveness of the public realm. In some cases (Bristol being an example) councils employ people specifically to strategically manage the city-centre public spaces. Public art officers could also potentially improve the quality of life in public space, particularly if their remit could extend to the promotion of street entertainment and impromptu cultural activities rather than just visual art.

Good public space management is about more than making places safe and crime-free; it should also be proactive in several ways, encouraging or initiating interesting activities, ensuring adequate maintenance and repair of the physical fabric and initiating micro-adjustments in the light of observable use.

Taking the latter point first, town-centre managers and others responsible for the ongoing management of public space, unlike architects, urban designers and planners (who produce their designs and then walk away), have an interest in the day-to-day and long-term viability of spaces. They are therefore well placed to make or request the necessary adjustments and modifications that are inevitably necessary during the lifespan of any public space. Examples might be realignment of footpaths to reflect 'desire lines', provision of extra litter bins and benches in certain locations, adjusting signage or incorporating new planting. In fact public spaces can fail, or fail to meet their full potential, because nobody takes a holistic view of how they can be modified according to use and needs. It is highly unlikely that, in the case of new public spaces, the designers will have got every detail right at first, yet there is rarely any budget or allowance made for post-occupancy evaluation and subsequent modifications.

However durable the fabric of a public space is, it will inevitably deteriorate over time as a result of wear and tear and vandalism, unless it is regularly and consistently maintained. Quick repairs not only show that a place is cared for, but will often thwart further deterioration (Kelling and Coles 1996). One example is offensive graffiti and tagging – speedy removal (possibly with the application of anti-graffiti coatings) has been shown to deter further spraying, as offenders do not have the time to celebrate their markings. If damaged street furniture is not fixed, further damage will escalate, as the environment deteriorates into a free-for-all target for destruction (see Zimbardo 1973). Even something as relatively simple (yet so often neglected) as regularly emptying litter bins and clearing up strewn rubbish can have a crucial effect on the quality and perception of public spaces. The problem here is often that, in the absence of people such as park keepers, no one is actually monitoring and then reacting to the overall condition of public spaces on a daily basis.

In Denmark, Germany and other continental European countries, there is a continuing traditional trade of 'streetbuilder' (*Strassenbauer* in German) – someone skilled in all the interconnected elements of maintaining public outdoor space. In the UK there is generally no such urban caretaker who has overall responsibility for the upkeep of the urban realm, with the result that maintenance and upgrading is fragmented and incoherent, with some aspects, such as the removal of redundant signs and equipment, being neglected altogether (CABE Space 2007). This is compounded by the UK custom of providing funding for capital expenditure, such as water features, fancy lighting and public artworks, with very little provision for long-term ongoing maintenance, resulting in the deterioration of many promising features (Brand 1994, Gallacher 2005).

Figure 155 St Mark's Square, Venice

The final point about management (also mentioned earlier, page 120) is the potential of public space managers to create or facilitate lively and intriguing activity – sometimes known as 'animation' of spaces. This can be as simple as licensing or allowing street entertainers and vendors, or as complex as organizing large public events such as fairs and festivals.

Although free festivals in public spaces need subsidizing, this can often be justified and achieved as a result of the extra economic benefits they bring to the town (through more visitors staying and spending). However, many of these animations need not cost very much and may indeed be self-funding. For example, a soup festival in Krakow, Poland, fills the squares and streets of the Jewish Quarter simply as a result of all the local cafes and restaurants offering free soup. They make up any losses by the substantially increased sale of drinks and other food. Free music from buskers and local bands adds to the ambience. Another example is the 'Streets Alive' event held annually in Bristol, where environmental groups are allowed to reclaim selected streets and turn them into 'living rooms' for the day.

All in all, the way public spaces are managed and animated is as important as design and location in the creation and maintenance of conviviality in the public realm.

Figure 156 Folklore festival in central square, Viana de Castelo, northern Portugal

Figure 157 Streets Alive festival, Bristol

Case Study: Padua

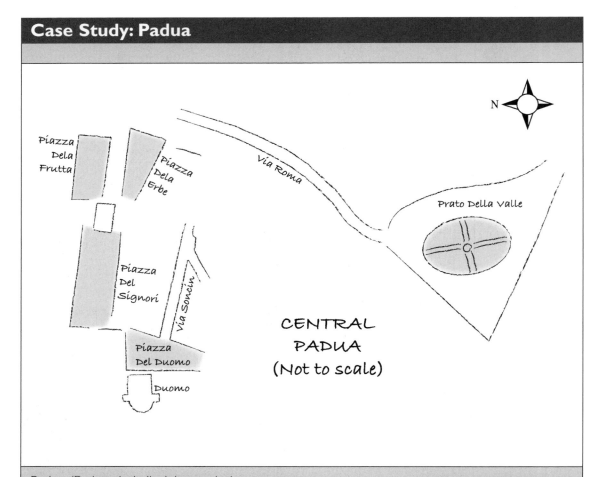

Padua (Padova in Italian) is a typical medium-sized city (about 400,000 population in the greater urban area) in the Veneto region of Northern Italy. It has a series of classic Italian piazza in the historic central area and an extensive programme of pedestrianization that has made it into a very people-friendly city. However, enlightened urban space planning has not reached out to the suburbs where some of the new public spaces are as dismal as anywhere in Europe.

Figure 158 Piazza dei Signori: one of a series of linked central squares

Figures 159 and 160 Prato della Valle, one of Europe's largest urban squares, was a place better known in Padua for drug dealing and other antisocial activities until overgrown vegetation was removed and tree crowns were raised. It is now a safe and successful gathering place both by day and night

Figures 161 and 162 Many central streets have been pedestrianized, with cafes and bookstalls taking over the spaces formerly occupied by vehicles (Via Soncin, above; Via Roma, below)

Outside the central area, public spaces rapidly lose their conviviality.

Figure 163 This plaza in front of a new development on the edge of the historic centre could be anywhere and is used by no one

Figures 164 and 165 Public space in the Selvazzano suburb of Padua has been virtually abandoned – not surprising when the local authority has erected a sign forbidding almost every kind of playful activity

Case Study: York

York Minster

King Square

Newgate Market

St. Sampson's Square

Parliament Square

St. Mary's Square

CENTRAL
YORK
(Not to scale)

St. Helen's Square

RIVER OUSE

Mansion House

York has a population of 180,000 and is a historic city – where the Viking and Roman settlements were overlaid by a medieval street pattern that forms the basis of the current layout within the city walls. As an ancient market and administrative centre it has an abundance of central public spaces. Most of these spaces have been in situ for hundreds of years, but one new space, St Mary's Square, has been created and appears to be successful, nestling as it does among a mixture of old buildings and some reasonably sympathetic new ones. York has the benefit of being a tourist destination and thus can sustain a high level of street animation, although it should be pointed out that all but one of its central squares predate the tourist influx.

Figures 166 and 167 Trampolining and busking in Parliament Square

Figures 168 and 169 King Square

As with so many other historic cities, public spaces in the areas of new development (see, for example, Figure 75 on page 72) have been much less successful than in the historic core. It may be that, as illustrated in the Glasgow experiment described by Gallacher (2005), public space can only be truly successful in dense, mixed-use urban cores. This is borne out in York, where the new St Mary's Square in the heart of the old town has proved to be a convivial space.

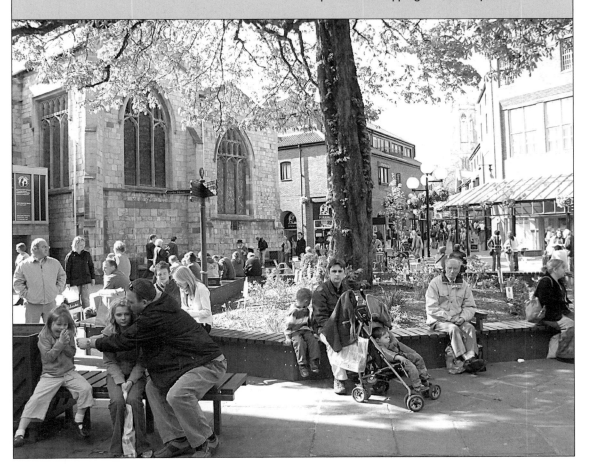

Figure 170 St Mary's Square: a new space and part of the Coppergate redevelopment

The Constituents of Conviviality

This section aims to pull together and summarize many of the points raised earlier in the book.

I suggest that there is no single blueprint for a convivial space, but successful spaces do seem to share some common elements. These may be broadly categorized under the headings of *physical* (including design and practical issues), *geographical*, *managerial* and *psychological and sensual* (how the space affects our mind, spirit and senses). As with most attempts at categorization, there is some overlap as some elements may be listed under more than one category; so in order to create some order out of an otherwise random list, the elements are categorized as follows:

Physical

- **Plenty of sitting places** (not necessarily formal fixed benches)
- **Good quality and robust** – successful public spaces will get a lot of wear and tear. Investing in high quality, durable materials will save money in the long term
- **Adaptable** (both for different uses and over time) – organic, incremental, fine-grained development copes with the inevitable changes affecting public space and allows it to go on thriving
- **Asymmetrical, yet well proportioned** (balance without symmetry) – most successful public spaces are not completely rectilinear, often because they have grown and evolved in response to the topography and dynamics of the surrounding area
- **Variety and intriguing details** (i.e. not monolithic) – this should comprise interesting landscaping, including plants, shrubs and trees, and intriguing use of colour and/or texture on built vertical surfaces
- **Carefully considered and appropriate horizontal surface treatments** – for both practical and aesthetic reasons; these are particularly important where there are changes in level, in order that no one should be disadvantaged by their physical ability or needs
- **Not too large** – or too small!

Geographical

- **Location** (urban core, neighbourhood or suburb) – generally public spaces work best when they are reasonably central, either in a town or neighbourhood, and are at the convergence of routes that people use for other purposes. They also work better when they are surrounded by mixed uses rather than monocultures such as offices or housing

- **Type of neighbourhood and surrounding areas** – new public spaces are sometimes used to attempt to regenerate downtown or formerly problematic areas. However, if the immediate surroundings are still perceived as unsafe or neglected, people are unlikely to go there or run the risk of lingering there
- **Clusters, sequences and strings of spaces** – as the case studies show, many of the most successful urban cores have more than one public space, allowing for variety of use and the pleasure of moving through a cityscape
- **Relation to transport** (motorized and pedestrian routes) – unless they are just for people living in the immediate surroundings, good public spaces will need to be easily accessible by all means of transport, but should not be dominated by their presence

Managerial

- **Diversity of use** – people need a variety of reasons to gather and linger
- **Promotion of a relaxed, round-the-clock culture** – there is a fine balance to attain between ensuring security and imposing excessive surveillance that makes people feel uncomfortable – on

the whole people are good at policing themselves, so the best management encourages a variety of people to be using the space at all times. There needs to be sufficient but not oppressive supervision so that crime risk and incivilities are kept under control

- **Inclusiveness** – ideally everyone should feel welcome in a good public space, even if parts of it have dedicated group activities (such as play spaces or skateboarding opportunities)
- **Well maintained and clean** – a place that is obviously cared for will be much more popular than one that looks neglected. Lack of adequate maintenance also leads to 'tipping': an escalation of damage and deterioration (e.g. graffiti tagging that is not swiftly removed will encourage more; if rubbish is not cleared up promptly, users will not hesitate to dump more)
- **Vehicular circulation banned or tightly controlled**
- **Adequately lit**
- **Animation** – there should be opportunities for plenty of human activity, such as stalls, busking, skateboarding, picnicking, as people attract people. These mixed activities should be encouraged rather than deterred

Psychological and sensual

- **Human scale** – people seem to enjoy a sense of enclosure without feeling claustrophobic. Huge structures (whether they be walls or buildings) and vast open spaces may be awe-inspiring, but they are unlikely to facilitate a feeling of conviviality

- **Individuality and uniqueness** – places with distinctive character and identity become positively memorable and may attract repeat visits. People will have the sense that they are in a unique place. This will result in a space that is complex, but coherent

- **Feeling of safety** (unthreatening) – this can be achieved through design *and* the management of the space, and is also perceived by observing the behaviour of others

- **Comfortable microclimate** – both sun and shade and protection from cold winds (but encouragement of cooling breezes in hot climates!)

- **Visually satisfactory** – not too dazzling or gloomy

- **Incorporation of natural elements** (e.g. plants, trees, water)

- **Acoustically pleasant** – not too much mechanical noise (so you can talk), but not so quiet that you can be overheard

- **No bad smells** – preferably pleasant aromas (such as coffee, fresh baking or flowers)

- **Opportunities to eat and drink** – self-catering and purchasable

I am not suggesting that to qualify as a completely convivial space all the above elements should be present, but a high proportion of them contribute to the spaces I have observed as working well. Furthermore, the way in which these qualities combine to please the human consciousness is not an exact science. There are clearly some *objective* considerations, such as even paved surfaces, seating or 'loitering' locations, adequate lighting, amenable microclimate and safety from motor traffic. However, beyond these are many subjective effects that the design, layout and animation of a place may have on the degree of personal comfort and delight.

Different people will be affected by different combinations of elements to some extent, but there appears to be a core set of attributes that will please more or less anyone. The nearest analogy might be the experience of a good novel, movie or piece of music – everybody has different tastes, but there is wide agreement about which are the classics. Indeed, many of the bullet points above could, metaphorically, be applied to quality literature, cinema or music.

Finally, here are some very practical and specific things that the designers and maintainers of public spaces can do and avoid doing, in order to achieve the best possible spaces:

Do:
- design the open spaces at the same time as you design or redesign the buildings and other structures, rather than regarding the space as what's left over after the buildings have gone up
- design with safety and security in mind
- consider the effect of the space on all the senses (and not just visually)
- consult residents or potential users (all age groups). What do they like and dislike? What problems do they perceive? What do they want? What would they like to change?
- follow 'desire lines' for footpaths (it may be necessary to do this retrospectively)
- provide a variety of sitting opportunities (not just fixed benches)
- think about the microclimate and provide protection and shelter as appropriate
- provide opportunities and facilities for people to eat and drink
- encourage 'animation' of the space through activities, formal or informal
- define open spaces with trees clear stemmed up to 3.5m. Plant specially prepared trees of suitable species (Advance Nursery Stock) at a minimum size of 14–16cm girth. Use support stakes and metal bar or grille protectors in vulnerable locations

- minimize the use of shrubs, but if necessary use species with a maximum mature height of 1.0m
- use see-through metal bar fencing (if barriers are needed)
- apply anti-graffiti coatings to accessible vertical surfaces in vulnerable locations
- consider having 'graffiti walls' and community noticeboards
- consider having a range of designated spaces for different age groups (e.g. play spaces, sports equipment, youth shelters, benches and picnic or barbeque facilities), but make sure that they are linked and oversee each other
- install pedestrian-friendly lighting (mounted not too high and incorporating full colour spectrum luminaries)
- have litter bins adjacent to benches, picnic tables and shelters, and ensure they are emptied regularly
- have a rapid response system to clear up dumping, graffiti, fly-posting and vandalism
- put in place systems for regular greenery maintenance and rubbish removal
- have public toilet facilities on site or accessible nearby
- use the highest quality materials, fittings and plants that the budget can afford (they will save money in the long term)

Don't:
- put public spaces in isolated or low-density locations
- design spaces that result in entrapment spots or poor surveillance
- put too many restrictions on the use of public space

- ▨ use low-cost or high-maintenance materials
- ▨ add features (such as public art) that will rapidly deteriorate or break down
- ▨ install hardware that invites vandalism (e.g. flimsy street furniture or light fittings and any kind of slatted or plank timber fencing)
- ▨ use raised planters for shrubs or trees (they tend to get damaged and don't collect enough surface rainwater)
- ▨ use mass planting of grey or dull, dark green leafy shrubs (they're depressing)
- ▨ plant clusters of shrubs or plants that trap litter and make litter difficult to remove
- ▨ plant trees with a mature height of less than 10m, where casual surveillance is required
- ▨ plant flimsy trees (e.g. mountain ash or small cherries) – they either won't survive or won't thrive
- ▨ apply textured pebble-dash-type finishes to walls and accessible vertical surfaces (people can still spray graffiti on to them, which is then a nightmare to remove)
- ▨ plant protruding pebbles or stones into horizontal concrete surfaces (what's the point? – yet you find them in many urban locations as a cheap way to discourage foot passage)
- ▨ use single-leaf brickwork or blockwork for walls and external divisions (they will eventually get pulled down)
- ▨ put public benches too close to occupied buildings (they will provoke noise complaints from residents) or in locations where they are exposed from behind

There is no standard formula for creating convivial spaces, but many of the above dos and don'ts will help. It is important to remember that although design is important, the size and location of the space along with the way it is managed and animated are equally important factors. We have much to learn from the successful places of the past. Although we have many new technologies and the world has changed spectacularly in the last 100 years, the basic human need for conviviality has endured. It is no coincidence that most of the world's most popular public spaces have been there for hundreds of years (with some adaptation over time) – see, for example, Figures 5, 155 and 171.

With our current knowledge it should be possible to create new convivial urban spaces for our expanding cities, as well as improving those which haven't quite worked, by respecting the experience of history, yet not slavishly imitating what has gone before.

Figure 171 Grande Place, Brussels

References and Bibliography

Aasen B (2002) *Urban Squares*. Birkhauser, Basel, Switzerland

Abley S and Hill E (2004) *Designing Living Streets*. Living Streets, London

Alexander C (1977) *A Pattern Language*. Oxford University Press

Alexander C (1979) *The Timeless Way of Building*. Oxford University Press, New York

Alexander C (1987) *New Theory of Urban Design*. Oxford University Press

Alexander C (2004a) *The Nature of Order*. Vols 1–4. Center for Environmental Structure, Berkeley, CA

Alexander C (2004b) *Sustainability and Morphogenesis: The birth of a living world*. Schumacher Lecture, Bristol, October 30. Centre for Environmental Structure, Berkeley, CA

Andersson T (2002) 'Every Space has a Place', in Aasen B (ed.) *Urban Squares*. Birkhauser, Basel, Switzerland

Appleyard D (1981) *Livable Streets*. University of California Press, Berkeley, CA

Armitage R (2000) *Evaluation of Secured by Design Housing in West Yorkshire*. Home Office Briefing Note 7/00, Home Office, London

Atkinson R and Blandy S (2006) *Gated Communities: An international perspective*. Taylor and Francis, London

Bacon E (1975) *Design of Cities*. Thames & Hudson, London

Bentley I, Alcock A, Murrain P, McGlynn S and Smith G (1985) *Responsive Environments: A manual for designers*. Architectural Press, London

Bianchini F (1994) 'Night Cultures, Night Economies'. *Town and Country Planning*, November

Billingham J and Cole R (2002) *The Good Place Guide: Urban design in Britain and Ireland*. Batsford, London

Bloomer K and Moore C (1977) *Body, Memory and Architecture*. Yale University Press

Boudon P (1969) *Lived-in Architecture: Le Corbusier's Passac revisited*. Lund Humphries, London

Brand S (1994) *How Buildings Learn: What happens after they're built*. Penguin, New York

Brereton F, Clinch J P and Ferreira S (2006) *Happiness, Geography and the Environment*. Planning and Environmental Policy Research Series Working Paper. University College, Dublin

Bunschoten R (2002) *Public Spaces*. Black Dog Publishing, London

CABE (2004a) *Manifesto for Better Public Spaces*. Commission for Architecture and the Built Environment, London

CABE Space (2004b) *Please Walk on the Grass: The value of public space*. CABE, London

CABE Space (2004c) *Does Money Grow on Trees?* CABE, London

CABE Space (2005) *Decent Parks? Decent Behaviour? The link between the quality of parks and user behaviour*. CABE, London

CABE Space (2007) *This Way to Better Streets: Lessons from 10 successful streets*. CABE, London

Canter D (1974) *Psychology for Architects*. Applied Science Publishers, London

Canter D (1977) *The Psychology of Place.* Architectural Press, London

Carmona M, Heath T, Oc T and Tiesdell S (2003) *Public Places – Urban Spaces.* Architectural Press, Oxford

Carr S, Francis M, Rivlin L and Stone A (1992) *Public Space.* Cambridge University Press

Coleman A (1985) *Utopia on Trial.* Hilary Shipman, London

Comedia (1991) *Out of Hours: A study of the economics and life of town centres.* Gulbenkian Foundation

Cooper Marcus C and Francis C (1998) *People Places: Design guidelines for urban open space.* Van Nostrand Reinhold, New York

Coventry Safer Cities Project (1992) *City Centre Community Strategy.* Home Office Safer Cities Report, Home Office, London

Crouch S, Shaftoe H and Fleming R (1999) *Design for Secure Residential Environments.* Longman, Harlow

Cullen G (1961) *Townscape.* Architectural Press, London

Davis M (1992) *City of Quartz.* Verso, London

Design Council and RTPI (1979) *Streets Ahead.* Design Council, London

DoE (Department of the Environment) (1993) *Crime Prevention on Council Estates.* HMSO, London

Dryfoos J (1990) *Adolescents at Risk: Prevalence and prevention.* Oxford University Press, New York

Duany A and Plater-Zyberk E (1991) *Towns and Town Making Principles.* Rizzoli, New York

Duttmann M, Schmuck F and Uhl J (1981) *Color in Townscape.* Architectural Press, London

Ellin N (ed.) (1997) *Architecture of Fear.* Princeton Architectural Press, New York

Evans R (2006) 'Common Ground', *Urban Design,* Issue 97, Winter, pp31–33

Farbstein J and Kantrowitz M (1978) *People in Places: Experiencing, using and changing the built environment.* Prentice-Hall, NJ

Felson M and Clarke R (1998) *Opportunity Makes the Thief: Practical theory for crime prevention.* Police Research Series Paper 98. Home Office, London

Flierl B (2002) 'Public Space: Goods for sale', in Aasen B (ed.) *Urban Squares.* Birkhauser, Basel, Switzerland

Florida R (2005) *Cities and the Creative Class.* Routledge, New York

Fyfe N and Bannister J (1998) 'The Eyes Upon the Street: Closed circuit television surveillance and the city', in Fyfe N (ed.) *Images of the Street: Planning, identity and control in public space.* Routledge, London

Gallacher P (2005) *Everyday Spaces: The potential of neighbourhood space.* Thomas Telford, London

Garmory N and Tennant R (2005) *Spaced Out: A guide to award-winning contemporary spaces in the UK.* Architectural Press, Oxford

Gehl J (2003) *Life Between Buildings: Using public space.* Danish Architectural Press, Copenhagen

Gehl J and Gemzoe L (1996) *Public Spaces: Public life.* Danish Architectural Press, Copenhagen

Gehl J and Gemzoe L (2001) *New City Spaces.* Danish Architectural Press, Copenhagen

Gold J and Revill G (eds) (2000) *Landscapes of Defence.* Prentice Hall, Harlow, England

Goodchild S and Owen J (2007) 'What Happened to Childhood? – How we are failing the young'. *The Independent,* London, 10 June

Goodman R (1972) *After the Planners.* Penguin, Harmondsworth

Graham J and Smith D (1994) *Diversion from Offending: The role of the Youth Service.* Crime Concern, Swindon

Greed C (2003) *Inclusive Urban Design: Public toilets.* Architectural Press, Oxford

Greenspace Scotland (2004) *Making the Links: Greenspace and the quality of life.* Greenspace Scotland, Stirling

Guite H, Clark C and Ackrill G (2006) 'The impact of the physical and urban environment on mental well-being', *Journal of the Royal Institute of Public Health,* no 120, pp1117–1126

Hall D (1997) *The Dufferin Papers.* Marathon Realty Company Limited, Toronto

Halpern D (1995) *More than Bricks and Mortar? Mental health and the built environment,* Taylor and Francis, London

Hamdi N (2004) *Small Change: About the art of practice and the limits of planning in cities.* Earthscan, London

Hampshire R and Wilkinson M (2002) *Youth Shelters and Sports Systems: a good practice guide* (2nd edition). Thames Valley Police

Hillier B and Hanson J (1984) *The Social Logic of Space.* Cambridge University Press

Hirschfield A and Bowers K (1997) 'The Effect of Social Cohesion on Levels of Recorded Crime in Disadvantaged Areas', *Urban Studies,* vol 34, no 8, pp1275–1295

Holland C, Clark A, Katz G and Peace S (2007) *Social Interactions in Urban Public Spaces.* Joseph Rowntree Foundation, York

Hough M (1989) *City Form and Natural Process.* Routledge, London

Jacobs A (1993) *Great Streets.* MIT Press, Cambridge, MA

Jacobs A and Appleyard D (1987) 'Towards an Urban Design Manifesto', *Journal of the American Planning Association,* no 53, pp112–120

Jacobs J (1961) *The Death and Life of Great American Cities: The failure of town planning.* Random House, New York

Jerde J (1998) 'Capturing the leisure zeitgeist – creating places to be', *Architectural Design,* Profile #131. Architectural Design, London

Kaplan R and Kaplan S (1989) *The Experience of Nature: A psychological perspective.* Cambridge University Press

Kaplan R, Kaplan S and Ryan R (1998) *With People in Mind: Design and management of everyday nature.* Island Press, Washington DC

Kayden J (2005) 'Using and Misusing Law to Design the Public Realm', in Ben-Joseph E and Szold T (eds) *Regulating Place.* Routledge, New York

Kellert S R and Wilson E O eds (1993) *The Biophilia Hypothesis.* Island Press, Washington DC

Kelling G and Coles C (1996) *Fixing Broken Windows: Restoring order and reducing crime in our communities.* The Free Press, New York

King M (1988) *Making Social Crime Prevention Work: The French experience.* NACRO, London

Kliczkowski M (2003) *Friedensreich Hundertwasser.* Loft Publications, Barcelona

KPMG/SNU (1990) *Counting Out Crime: The Nottingham Crime Audit.* Nottingham Safer Cities Project

Krier R (1979) *Urban Space.* Academy Editions, London

Landry C (2006) *The Art of City Making.* Earthscan, London

Layard R (2005) *Happiness: Lessons from a new science.* Allen Lane, London

Le Corbusier (1943) *Charte d'Athènes* [*Athens Charter*], Plon, Paris

Leier M (2004) *100 Most Beautiful Squares of the World.* Rebo, Lisse, Netherlands

Lennard S and Lennard H (1995) *Livable Cities Observed: A source book of images and ideas.* Gondolier Press, Carmel, CA

Llewelyn-Davis (2005) *Urban Design Compendium.* English Partnerships and the Housing Corporation, London

Lynch K (1960) *The Image of the City.* MIT Press, Cambridge, MA

Lynch K (1971) *Site Planning.* MIT Press, Cambridge, MA

Lyon D (1993) 'An Electrical Panopticon? A social critique of surveillance theory', *Sociological Review,* vol 41, no 4, pp653–678

Madanipour A (1996) *Design of Urban Space: An inquiry into socio-spatial process.* Wiley, Chichester

Mahnke F (1987) *Color Environment and Human Response.* Van Nostrand Reinhold, New York

Marsh P (1990) *Lifestyle: Your surroundings and how they affect you.* Sidgwick & Jackson, London

Mean M and Tims C (2005) *People Make Places: Growing the public life of cities.* Demos, London

Montgomery J (1994) 'The evening economy of cities', *Town and Country Planning,* November

Moore R (1986) *Childhood's Domain: Play and place in child development.* Croom Helm, London

Morgan R and Newburn T (1997) *The Future of Policing.* Routledge, London

Morris D (1978) *Manwatching: A field guide to human behaviour.* Jonathan Cape, London

Moughtin C (1992) *Urban Design: Street and square.* Butterworth, Oxford

Moughtin C, Cuesta R, Sarris C and Signoretta P (1999) *Urban Design: Method and techniques.* Architectural Press, Oxford

Mumford L (1964) *The Highway and the City.* Secker & Warburg, London

National Centre for Social Research (1998) *The 1998 Youth Lifestyles Survey.* NCSR, London

National Heart Forum, Living Streets and CABE (2007) *Building Health: Creating and enhancing places for healthy, active lives.* NHF, London

Neal P (ed.) (2003) *Urban Villages and the Making of Communities.* Spon Press, London

ODPM (2002) *Cleaner, Safer, Greener.* Office of the Deputy Prime Minister, London

ODPM (2005) *Planning Policy Statement 1: Delivering sustainable development.* Office of the Deputy Prime Minister, London

ODPM/Home Office (2004) *Safer Places: The planning system and crime prevention.* Thomas Telford Publishers, Tonbridge

Percy-Smith B and Matthews H (2001) 'Tyrannical Spaces: Young people, bullying and urban neighbourhoods', *Local Environment,* vol 6, no 1, pp49–63

Poole R (1994) *Operation Columbus: Travels in North America.* West Midlands Police, Birmingham

Prak N (1977) *The Visual Perception of the Built Environment.* Delft University Press

Ramsay M (1989) *Downtown Drinkers: The perceptions and fears of the public in a city centre.* Crime Prevention Unit Paper 19. Home Office, London

Ramsay M (1990) *Lagerland lost? An experiment in keeping drinkers off the street in central Coventry.* Home Office Crime Prevention Unit Paper 22. Home Office, London

Rapoport A (1977) *Human Aspects of Urban Form: Towards a man-environment approach to urban form and design.* Pergamon, Oxford

Rapoport A (1990) *The Meaning of the Built Environment.* University of Arizona Press, AZ

Rasmussen S E (1959) *Experiencing Architecture.* Chapman and Hall, London

Rossi A (1982) *The Architecture of the City.* MIT Press, MA

Rowe C and Koetter F (1978) *Collage City.* MIT Press, MA

Rowland K (1966) *The Shape of Towns.* Ginn & Co, London

Rudofsky B (1964) *Architecture without Architects: A short introduction to non-pedigreed architecture.* Academy Editions, London

Safe Neighbourhoods Unit (1993) *Not Afraid to Trade: Business and crime prevention in Hackney.* SNU, London

Sampson R, Raudenbush S and Earls F (1997) 'Neighbourhoods and Violent Crime: A multilevel study of collective efficacy', *Science,* vol 277, pp918–924

Saville G (1996) *Selected Topics in Environmental Criminology.* International CPTED Association, US

Sennett R (1973) *The Uses of Disorder: Personal identity and city life.* Penguin, Harmondsworth

Sennett R (1986) *The Fall of Public Man.* Faber & Faber, London

Sennett R (1994) *Flesh and Stone.* Faber & Faber, London

Shaftoe H (1998) 'Planning for Crime Prevention', in Greed C and Roberts M (eds) *'Introducing Urban Design.* Longman, Harlow, Essex

Shaftoe H (2000) 'Community Safety and Actual Neighbourhoods', in Barton H (ed.) *Sustainable Communities*. Earthscan, London

Shaftoe H (2002) 'The Camera Never Lies but, in Truth, is it any Use?', *The Community Safety Journal*, vol 1, no 2, Autumn

Shaftoe H (2004) *Crime Prevention: Facts, fallacies and the future*. Palgrave Macmillan, Basingstoke

Shaftoe H and Read R (2005) 'Planning out Crime: The appliance of science or an act of faith?', in Tilley N (ed.) *'Handbook of Crime Prevention and Community Safety'*. Willan Publishing, Cullompton, Devon

Smith P (1974) *The Dynamics of Urbanism*. Hutchinson, London

Stickland R (1996) *The Twenty Four Hour City Concept: An appraisal of its adoption and its social and economic viability*. Department of Urban Planning, University of Nottingham

Taylor, N (2008) 'Legibility and Aesthetics in Urban Design' *Journal of Urban Design*, vol 13 (forthcoming)

Thomsen C (1998) *Sensuous Architecture*. Prestel, Munich

Tibbalds F (1989) 'Review of "A Vision of Britain"', *Town Planning Review*, vol 60, no 4, pp465–467

Tibbalds F (1992) *Making People-friendly Towns*. Longman, Harlow, Essex

Town S and O'Toole R (2005) 'Crime Friendly Neighbourhoods: Are new urbanists sacrificing safety?', *Reason* (Los Angeles), Feb, pp30–36

Turner J (1976) *Housing by People: Towards autonomy in building environments*. Marion Boyars, London

Turner T (1996) *City as Landscape: A post-modern view of design and planning*. Spon Press, London

Urban Task Force (1999) *Towards an Urban Renaissance: Final report of the Urban Task Force*. Department for the Environment, Transport and the Regions, London

van Leeuwen T and Jewitt C, (2001) *Handbook of Visual Analysis*. Sage Publications, London

Vergara C (1995) *The New American Ghetto*. Rutgers University Press, NJ

Waiton S (2001) 'Scared of the Kids? – Curfews, crime and the regulation of young people'. Sheffield Hallam University, School of Cultural Studies

Walljasper I (2007) *The Great Neighborhood Book*. New Society Publishers, British Columbia, Canada

Ward C (1974) *Human Space: Utopia*. Penguin Education, Harmondsworth

Ward C (1989) *Welcome, Thinner City: Urban survival in the 1990s*. Bedford Square Press, London

Ward Thompson C and Travlou P (eds) (2007) *Open Space: People space*. Taylor & Francis, London

Watson D, Plattus A and Shibley R (eds) (2003) *Time-saver Standards for Urban Design*. McGraw-Hill, New York

Wekerle G (1999) 'From Eyes on the Street to Safe Cities', *Places*, Fall edition

Welsh B and Farrington D (2002) *Crime Prevention Effects of Closed Circuit Television: A systematic review*. Home Office Research Study 252. Home Office RDS Directorate, London

White R (1998) *Public Spaces for Young People: A guide to creative projects and positive strategies*. National Crime Prevention Program, Attorney-General's Department, Australia

Whyte W (1980) *The Social Life of Small Urban Spaces*. Project for Public Spaces, New York

Whyte W (1988) *City: Rediscovering the Centre*. Anchor/Doubleday, New York

Williams K, Johnstone C and Goodwin M (2000) 'CCTV Surveillance in Urban Britain: Beyond the rhetoric of crime prevention', in Gold J and Revell G (eds) *Landscapes of Defence*. Prentice Hall, Harlow

Wilson, E O (1984) *Biophilia*. Harvard University Press, Cambridge, MA

Wood D (1981) 'In Defense of Indefensible Space', in Brantingham P J and Brantingham P

L (eds) *Environmental Criminology*. Waveland Press, IL

Woolley H (2003) *Urban Open Spaces*. Spon Press, London

Worpole K (1992) *Towns for People*. Open University Press, Buckingham

Worpole K and Greenhalgh L (1996) *The Freedom of the City*. Demos, London

Worpole K and Knox K (2007) *The Social Value of Public Spaces*. Joseph Rowntree Foundation, York

Yi-Fu Tuan (1977) *Space and Place: The perspective of experience*. University of Minnesota Press

Young J (1998) 'Zero Tolerance: Back to the future', in Marlow M and Pitts J (eds) *Planning Safer Communities*. Russell House Publishing, Lyme Regis

Zimbardo P (1973) 'A Field Experiment in Auto-Shaping', in Ward C (ed.) *Vandalism*. Architectural Press, London

Internet Resources

Three websites relating to this topic (the first British, the second European, the third American):

- **www.cabespace.org.uk** –the Commission for Architecture and the Built Environment (CABE) is a British quango charged with the task of improving the quality of design, primarily through advice and guidance.
- **www.spaceforpublic.org** – The European Centre on Public Space, modelled loosely on PPS (see below).
- **www.pps.org** –The Project for Public Spaces (PPS) is an independent American advisory and campaigning organization, that argues for the improved quality of life that accrues from good quality public spaces.

Index